CHASTITY

The Guide to Male Chastity

Marisa Rudder

Marisa Rudder

Author of Love & Obey, Real Men Worship Women, and Oral Sex
for Women

Available on Amazon Books.

Please contact: Marisa Rudder

Email: femaleledrelationshipbook@gmail.com

Printed in the United States of America Publisher's Cataloging-in-
Publication data

ISBN: 978-1-7361835-0-2

Dedication

I would like to dedicate this book to all the strong, brave ladies who have joined or about to join the Love & Obey movement and live a female led lifestyle and the supportive gentlemen who recognized the natural superiority of females. It is also my desire that women and men experience the joy, happiness, and passion from exploring all aspects of a loving Female Led Relationship (FLR) and understanding all the benefits of a loving female authority. If you have not already, please join us on social media.

You can find out more at our website:
www.loveandobey.com

Or follow me on social media:

FACEBOOK
https://www.facebook.com/femaleledrelationships

TWITTER
https://twitter.com/loveandobeybook

YOUTUBE
https://www.youtube.com/channel/UCkX3wmd934WR103 hStbzbiQ

INSTAGRAM
https://www.instagram.com/femaleledrelationships

WARNING

This book contains adult sexual content. It should not be read by anyone under the age of 18 years. In addition to sexually explicit and descriptive content, this book contains controversial sexual discussions about spanking, discipline and Female Led Relationships.

Introduction

Millions of chastity devices have been sold on Amazon in 2020. Chastity is searched 200,000 times a month on Google. Why all the fascination? What is chastity, and why is interest in it growing exponentially? Couples have reported that chastity and orgasm control has transformed their relationship or marriage, injecting excitement, adventure, and taking intimacy to a whole new level. Who would think that millions of men would crave wearing a chastity lock for days with their Queen holding the only key?

That's real trust and devotion. More couples have admitted to engaging in chastity and making it the focus in their relationships. Statistics don't lie. Male chastity is part of Female Led Relationships, and as the leader of the Love and Obey Female Led Movement, I can confirm that interest in a female taking the lead and the man becoming the supportive gentleman is expanding worldwide. Men contact every day and ask questions about how to serve their Queen correctly.

My five bestselling books are all geared to helping couples to wake up a dead marriage and inject some new life and purpose into relationships. Today, chastity takes female led to a whole new level.

In a Female Led Relationship, the desire to be controlled by a strong female becomes even more important. More women are taking control of many aspects of their lives and many are leading countries, governments, corporations, cities, households, and now the bedroom.

My previous books *Love & Obey* and *Real Men Worship Women* are blockbuster hits and provide the essential guidance that a couple needs to build a lasting, successful relationship. Part of keeping the relationship spark alive is controlling the focus of the man's desire on the Queen. Every woman knows that men are driven by sex. It's natural for them. It is a primitive urge that's impossible for men to ignore. It is programmed in their DNA from the dawn of time. The irresistible force of their libido is like a raging fire, burning up everything that stands in the way of its desire to consume. When you are in a relationship, you become the object of his desire. As part of a Female Led Relationship, controlling a man's orgasm is the ultimate control, and this could be why male chastity is growing exponentially.

In this book, we will discuss how chastity, coming out of an ancient practice of chaste pure life practices for centuries by monks, priests, and other spiritual individuals, has gained such notoriety and how it transforms a relationship or marriage. We will analyze how it fits into a Female Led Relationship and helps couples to build much deeper and more intimate connections. When a woman controls the main driving force of a man, she assumes ultimate control and he submits. This dramatically changes the dynamic of a relationship from patriarchal to female led. It is this transformation that has helped to save thousands of dead marriages and failing relationships, as reported by thousands of couples worldwide. People everywhere are eager and interested in chastity to the point where chastity devices are being sold in the millions. To show the popularity of male chastity even the Tech world has got in on the action creating app enables devices.

Why do men crave chastity? I believe that it goes back to their need for attention from a strong female. Fifty percent of marriages will end in divorce, which means a significant part of the population will be raised by women. Of the households with two parent families, many are experiencing a shift where the woman assumes control. So children, particularly men, will crave a strong dominant female like their mothers. "Men marry their mothers" refer to the idea that more men will choose a long-term partner who exhibits similar characteristics and may even resemble their mothers. I also believe that men crave the same discipline and attention that they received from a strong maternal figure. The Queen who places her man in Chastity has the ultimate control, and men love this. They succumb to a strong female because it keeps the focus on them. More focus on the relationship means a stronger relationship or marriage.

In the Female Led Relationships, more men have admitted that they enjoy and have a strong desire for their women to control them. For instance, placing a penis into a chastity lock where the Queen has the only key, is arousing in itself. Today, more relationships are being led by women. Women are taking charge in the household and in the bedroom. Men are loving the experience of being under the spell and the dominance of women and spanking just adds to the feeling of control for the Queen. When women feel empowered, then they are at their best and men get excited when they take charge and show their power. So it's a win-win for most.

This book will serve as an introduction to chastity, and it will provide a complete guide to engaging in this practice and use of male chastity devices. Added to an already healthy sex life, chastity can be a fun way to spice up the bedroom with so many additional ways to engage in sexual fantasy.

Table of Contents

CHAPTER 1

What is Male Chastity?

M ale chastity has become one of the biggest categories of interest in relationships and sexuality to explode in the last five years. There are more TV shows and scenes in movies depicting it, and if you search the chastity cage on Amazon, you'll see thousands of brands and devices available for sale. One brand reported over a million devices sold in the last twelve months. What that means is that millions of couples are obsessed with chastity. But why the fascination?

Chastity means abstinence. The man refrains from sexual intercourse or having an orgasm unless the Queen gives him permission. At first glance, this may seem like the most unnatural thing in the world. Some may even think, why would I want to stop my man's orgasm? This was my first thought when I was introduced to it, but after experience and an in-depth analysis, the true power of male chastity was revealed. Today, chastity has become a transformative experience for many relationships. At the source, and an important point for women to understand, is that when a man agrees to chastity, he is showing complete submission and devotion to his Queen, over and above any other undertaking in life. In addition, it gives the woman complete control over him. This is the ultimate sign of respect to the Queen, and it is essentially what transforms the relationship.

As part of a Female Led Relationship, male chastity becomes the major test and many couples have reported much more intimacy and a deepening of their bond after starting chastity. Male chastity may take many forms: using a physical locking device, the chastity cage, or none at all. It may involve orgasm control, semen ejaculation control, or simply no sexual gratification at all. Some men remain locked for hours, some for days. The length of time is determined by the Queen, but like all other practices in the relationship, there must still be consent from both partners.

Chastity is not to be used as a way to punish the man, although some couples enjoy the addition of spanking, bondage, and BDSM as additional methods of punishment. The real reason for chastity is to deepen the man's fixation on the Queen as the ultimate ruler of the relationship. She who holds the key to his lock has the ultimate control. As a sexual practice in the female led lifestyle, male chastity, in my opinion, is the crème de la crème. The Queen has the ultimate control, and she is the supreme leader.

For men, who are in a Female Led Relationship or craves being in one, giving the Queen this kind of control will be orgasmic in itself. It takes your arousal, sex, and daily life to a whole new level. It requires some sacrifice but the relationship is transformed and both of you will evolve. Ladies, you can encourage male chastity, without locking the male's penis in a chastity device but what the cage does, is it helps him to exert self-control over his sexual desires, for example, masturbating when he is alone or pressuring his woman into having sex "because he wants it" or cheating if he is with another woman.

Ladies, you are the Key Holder who holds the keys to her man's chastity cage. This makes you the "guardian" of his penis and his orgasms, and from this day forward, it will make you the focus of all his sexual desire. He will turn you into his sexual goddess in his mind. The man in chastity promises not to orgasm without permission, and there is a power exchange between them where the Key Holder now "owns" her man's penis. She alone decides when he can orgasm and when she alone can unlock his penis. She will control his orgasms as she sees fit, whether he is wearing the device or not.

This is basic male chastity. We will be exploring male chastity from the context of a Female Led Relationship. So why has Male chastity become hugely popular in Female Led Relationships in which the man submits to his Queen who determines when and if he is allowed to have an orgasm? Male chastity comes from the word "chaste," which means virtuous or pure from sexual intercourse. Male chastity was practiced around marriage for many cultures where the couple had to refrain from sex until married. Today, sex has become out of control. In today's society, sex has become commercialized, and it is treated as just another form of entertainment or even a pass time. It's all about pleasure, the hookup, and the thrill of the chase. Male chastity is the intentional refraining from sex, and it is portrayed as being repressive and restrictive, but in reality, it can represent power, strength, and the ultimate devotion.

By practicing male chastity, the man gains inner strength to control his sexual desires. The *Love & Obey* teachings on sexual male chastity is clear. Any sexual activity without the express permission of a man's loving female authority is strictly prohibited. The man should be focused on his woman's satisfaction, not on his own. One of the biggest challenges I encountered was that our entire sex life is built around the patriarchal view of sex and engaging in sex.

Women are often pressured to have the perfect body, the perfect breasts, and today, a large, perfectly round butt to turn on her man. Many young women have reported having to spend hours working on building their butt because it is what the man wants. Patriarchal sexual intercourse involves the man who is erect and penetrates the woman by thrusting for a few minutes until he has an orgasm. Maybe she also orgasms, maybe she does not. Sometimes, a woman may request to then pleasure herself with her vibrator as an alternative.

A Female Led Relationship is the opposite. Sex is for the Queen. The man focuses on the Queen's sexual arousal and attempts to heighten the experience with oral sex while he focuses on her having multiple orgasms. He delays his own orgasm until she is sufficiently satisfied. Male chastity takes this one step further, now the Queen controls when he can get aroused and if he will be able to penetrate her at all. This increases the excitement of sexual pleasure as it keeps the man's focus squarely on pleasing the Queen. Now she is insanely happier as she leads the relationship, and the man is happier because he knows she is focused on him and his desire is for her alone. Both partners are satisfied and this makes for a deeper more successful relationship or marriage.

This book will explore everything to do with male chastity and orgasm control. It will help to improve even the most mundane and boring sex life, enhance your man's stamina and performance, and ensure that you receive more orgasms than ever before as he learns that sex is for your pleasure. His pleasure comes from giving you pleasure. We will explore all the forms of male chastity including, orgasm denial, orgasms control and semen retention. We will discuss the tools available for safely engaging in male chastity in a relationship or marriage and how it fits perfectly into a Love and Obey Female Led Relationship.

Male chastity will empower women to take more responsibility and control in a man's life and it fulfills that secret desire of men to be 100 percent subservient to their Queen and to become her ultimate lover. Ladies and Gentlemen, get ready to take your relationship and sex life to a whole new level.

CHAPTER 2

Why Is Male Chastity Such a Turn On?

M ale chastity involves giving complete control to your Queen, and she ultimately makes all of the decisions. Why is it such a turn on? The Queen holds the key to the chastity device, and she controls orgasm, so why is it so fascinating? Male chastity originates from BDSM. What most beginners to BDSM need to understand is the effort and responsibility that comes with being a dominant or the simultaneous control and vulnerability that comes with being a submissive.

In a healthy BDSM relationship, all partners aim to please each other, and the submissive sets their own boundaries. The basis of a Sub-Dom relationship is fulfilling your partner's needs, providing them pleasure, and constantly communicating to ensure you're doing both well. Not only is it imperative that all partners feel safe and cared for, but everyone must also have a deep understanding of the other's boundaries, comfort levels, and sexual interests. This is true for male chastity where the Queen is the dominant and her man is the submissive. There are many things that couples try to do to improve the sex life and connection—they may go to counseling, have date night, try role-play, spanking, or swinging.

But all of these are focused on external, and none are aimed squarely at the pleasure point. Male chastity is focused on the power center of a man, allowing you, his Queen, to control that power center and is the ultimate submission by the man, which is to serve her needs. This is what makes it so powerful and arousing. To understand what happens with male chastity, and why it's such a turn on, it's important to look at what happens at a physiological level. We will analyze the sexual response cycle.

There are four stages in the sexual response cycle:

1. **Desire:** The initial excitement phase triggered by mental or physical stimuli with increased muscle tension, erect nipples, blood flow to genitals, vaginal lubrication, and pre-cum.

2. **Arousal:** This is the plateau phase with heightened sexual tension and sensitivity just before orgasm.

3. **Orgasm:** This is the forceful release of sexual tension resulting in muscle contractions and ejaculation; generally, only lasting a few seconds up to a minute.

4. **Resolution:** This is the state of recovery and return to normal state. Penises refract but continued stimulation in some vaginas can lead to multiple orgasms.

The desire phase is the first stage, and this is where there is an increase in muscle tension, blood flow to the genitals, erect nipples, and vaginal lubrication. Things are getting heated up and arousal begins. The arousal phase is where breathing, heart rate, and blood pressure significantly increase, the woman's clitoris becomes highly sensitive, the man's testicles retract into the scrotum, and muscle spasms may begin in the feet, face, and hands. It is here that orgasm denial can begin. You can start by teasing and denying any touching or further arousal. Keeping your partner at the height of their arousal phase for longer—without letting them reach the orgasm phase—can be enjoyable for both of you. This represents one type of chastity.

Once you have satisfied your tease and denial, it's time for the orgasm phase. This is typically the shortest of all the phases and consists of muscle contractions and ejaculation. In chastity, the Queen can deny the orgasm altogether or just prolong it as long as possible. Following an orgasm, the resolution phase allows the body to slowly return to its normal state. This phase often accompanies feelings of satisfaction, intimacy, and fatigue. If no more stimulation follows an orgasm, this phase will begin immediately. The brain releases a variety of chemicals when we feel lust and attraction. Lust stimulates the production of estrogen and testosterone in the body, which increases erotic feelings and behavior.

When feeling attracted to another person, our dopamine levels surge, which is the same chemical produced when we feel good, for instance, during sexual stimulation. The more you lust and want an orgasm, the more of these chemicals circulating to keep you focused on the object of your attention, which is the Queen who holds the key to your orgasm. It is these physiological responses that makes chastity so powerful because ultimately the man's whole physiological response during sex is controlled by the Queen.

Chastity is a turn on because it immediately injects a sense of excitement and sexual tension into the relationship each and every day. When both partners are engaged and focused on each other, with the Queen teasing and the man showing complete willpower and devotion by holding back the most powerful urge in the body, this creates a continuous feeling of heightened sexuality. Each day is exciting, rather than a feeling of boredom and monotony. Chastity is the furthest thing from boring, and it helps to refocus the couple's energy on themselves, which increases intimacy, communication, and connection in the relationship.

As a woman, the ultimate sign of control is to put a cage on your man. Even if it seems like fun and a distraction, it still centers the attention on him. In turn, he shows complete devotion to you as he is now yours. He submits to you controlling his every move. He can't go far and roam free with you having locked up his penis, and since you are the person who will hold the key to his freedom, you become his ultimate Queen Goddess and ruler. This control of a man's manhood is a major turn on for them.

The great philosopher Hegel said in his master-slave dialectic, "Desire plays a very important role." This philosopher stated that animals have a desire that is satisfied with an immediate object. The animal isn't aware of what it desires. However, this is different for human beings. For Hegel, history equals the history of social relations—two human desires are facing each other. What human beings really desire is to be desired by others. In other words, they want to be recognized by others. This means that human desire is fundamentally a yearning for recognition. Human beings want others to give them an autonomous value; a value that's their own and that makes them different from others. This is what defines the human condition.

Therefore, according to Hegel, the main characteristic of human beings is imposing themselves on others. This is why male chastity— with the Queen imposing her will on a man and all the focus is on him while he desires her and is turned on by her controlling him—is so powerful. It goes to the heart of the social condition. The desire part, like Hegel proposes, is a fundamental need for human beings.

Since the beginning of history, there have been dominators and dominated people. Due to that dominance, the master coerces the slave and forces him or her to work. However, the master ends up depending on the slave to be able to survive. But what is important here is that even though the master is in control and holds the power, the slave is indispensable. This applies to Female Led Relationships and chastity because many opponents will argue that the Queen has all the power, but in fact, it is the man who becomes invaluable as he serves her. She needs him more now, and he fulfills his position as the supportive gentleman.

Where Chastity takes this even further is the desire component. The basic human need is fulfilled, and the desire for the Queen and her desire to be served is what makes this so powerful for relationships. In my experience, it has the power to transform the relationship in ways, which could not be achieved by counseling, retreats, or any other method. Remember, power can be defined as the ability or capacity to direct or influence the behavior of others in a particular way. Power is not limited to domination and submission. Instead, power in relationships is understood to be the respective abilities of each person in the relationship to influence each other and direct the relationship—and this is a very complex element of romantic partnerships that is changing every day. More men want their women to have power over them. In same sex relationships, one partner always dominates.

CHAPTER 3

What is Male Orgasm Control?

Male orgasm control is the act of experiencing or allowing someone else to experience a high level of sexual arousal and pleasure for a long time without allowing an orgasm. This can be done with or without a male chastity device. For many, orgasm control is about the physical build up and release. For others, the psychological aspect of power, control, and giving in is the hotness. A submissive man is obedient and will do anything possible to not come until the dominant Queen gives permission or forces the orgasm. If the submissive isn't strong enough to hold the orgasm on their own, the Queen can stop the orgasm simply with a command. The fantasy of being controlled usually drives the intensity of the orgasm, coupled with anticipation and release that typically increases the strength of how the partner experiences the orgasm.

Orgasm control of your man allows you, the Queen, to experience a high level of sexual arousal and pleasure for a long time along with multiple orgasms, while not allowing the man any pleasure except the gratification he receives from pleasuring his woman. Over time, this trains the man to focus on the female's pleasure and be grateful for permission to ejaculate once in a while. It's an area of erotic experience for many in Female Led Relationships. Orgasm control also involves erotic sexual denial in which he is kept in a heightened state of sexual arousal for an extended length of time without being allowed an orgasm.

Erotic sexual denial has the power to strengthen your intimacy with your man and lead both of you to higher levels of sexual stimulation without allowing him to actually orgasm. In Female Led Relationships, the Queen is in charge and has all of the power to control her man. So, taking a dominant role and holding off his ejaculation for an extended time frame will give him toe-curling orgasms when you do finally take them over the edge and allow him to orgasm. Deliberately holding your man back from that explosive moment will lead to amplified erotic fantasies about you and heighten his anticipation of finally being unlocked and having sex with you—you will become his sex goddess.

Erotic sexual denial can last for short periods or long periods, or it may be used for those who really enjoy drawing out the anticipation of sexual intercourse until all other tasks or sexual acts are completed. Your man can remain locked at all times when all you desire is orgasming with oral sex stimulation. The only time to unlock your man is when you want penetration and the special satisfaction gained from sexual intercourse. All other times keep him locked, which can be minutes, days, weeks, or even months depending on your sexual desires. If you've been dying for more oral ladies, male chastity is one of the greatest ways to achieve this.

Every man needs to experience erotic orgasm denial. Prolonging that urge for an extended period of time can lead to dramatic amounts of sexual arousal and excitement. Prolonging the man's urge to explode goes a long way to helping the Queen to not only demonstrate her ultimate control, but he is trained to have willpower and self-control. The Queen becomes supreme leader when she controls the driving force in a man.

Even in infidelity, most men are not out just looking for pure sex. If this were the case, most men would be seeking a prostitute. When a man cheats, he is searching for that excitement and desire missing from his current relationship. With male chastity, the Queen can control his desire just by controlling his penis and his ability to have orgasms. So male chastity can also be used as a tool to wake up a dead sex life and re-focus the spotlight back on the Queen.

What is Semen Retention?

Semen retention is yet another form of male chastity and orgasm control. Not only can the orgasm be denied, but so too can ejaculation be avoided either through sexual abstinence or by practicing intercourse without ejaculation. Semen retention does not refer to the avoidance of male pleasure. In this practice, male pleasure is separated from ejaculation, making it possible for the man to enjoy the full pleasure of sexual intercourse without experiencing seminal ejaculation.

Semen retention is an ancient practice, believed to maximize male physical and spiritual energy. Much of the history appears to be rooted in Taoism. Worldwide, this practice exists in many cultures, under different names. Practitioners attribute near-mystical superpower qualities to semen conservation and the men who practice orgasm control rave about its benefits. They experience a notable boost in courage and self-confidence. More energy and focus and an increased attractiveness to women. This makes it a contributor to Male Chastity, because again, the focus is on the Queen. Some men claim to have greater mental clarity and awareness. And the motivation to do things that are good for men—like going to the gym, losing weight, increasing muscle mass, and sleeping better. They also claim to be more grounded and calmer. They say it boosts their sex drive, including harder erections, and they lose any erectile dysfunction that they had experienced.

Types of Orgasm Control

Orgasm control can also involve additional practices like edging, peaking, or surfing, and they are different from male orgasm denial. Although orgasm and ejaculation are delayed, they are eventually allowed at the end of each of these types of orgasm control. Orgasm denial prohibits men from ejaculating without the female partner's permission, but edging is where you bring your man right to the 'edge'—the brink of orgasm, only to stop or slow down stimulation just before reaching the climax. You are not completely denying the orgasm, you are prolonging the entire experience. Edging can be done through clitoral and genital stimulation, prostate massage, blowjob intercourse, or other various sexual acts— whatever gets your arousal into overload. Rile him up over and over until you finally allow him to let go. It will be intensely erotic for both partners, and often leads to feeling a much more intense and high-level orgasm.

Men become better versions of themselves when they are no longer constrained by selfish, male-focused, patriarchal sex. Once he can focus his attention on pleasing you, the Queen, every day of his life, he has a new purpose in life. He can work on succeeding at serving you, and that will only work to make you happier and increase the success of your marriage or Female Led Relationship. Think of how much fun it's going to be when every sex session is controlled and both of you are exploring raising arousal and your sexual enjoyment.

Avoidance of Masturbation

Avoidance of masturbation and porn is the simplest, and therefore perhaps the easiest first step in male chastity and orgasm control as well as semen retention. A well-trained man in chastity needs to learn to avoid both orgasms and ejaculation from masturbation while you administer more training during your sex sessions. This is one of the most important steps in male chastity as you will see in later chapters. Uncontrolled masturbation, uncontrolled is simply not allowed and must be restrained if he is to experience the real power of male chastity.

Orgasms and even semen are for the Queen only and not to be wasted with random sessions watching porn on his computer. Not only does masturbating while on the computer decrease his time focusing on you, but most men can become addicted, and they can eventually affect the sensitivity of his penis to arousal methods. This is similar to women addicted to their vibrators. Pretty soon, no amount of human methods can satisfy genitals that have been overstimulated with external methods. As a western society, we have allowed this to go on unchecked, but in male chastity, the foundation is to build self-control and submit to the woman's command.

Pull Out Method

The pull out method is considered yet another form of orgasm control, and this is where immediately before the man orgasms, he pulls his penis out of the vagina just before ejaculation. This was traditionally used as a method for birth control, but it is part of semen retention and thought of as orgasm control. As you will see later in the Love and Obey method of orgasm control, he pulls out, then performs oral sex on you until you orgasm.

CHAPTER **4**

What Are the Physiological Changes with Chastity?

The power of male chastity and orgasm control comes from the many physiological changes that occur in the body. There are scientifically based health benefits for men from orgasm denial and semen conservation. The five scientifically-measurable areas of impact on men are: an increase in testosterone levels, an increase in brain androgen receptors, a decrease in dopamine levels, a decrease in prolactin levels and an increase in serotonin levels. The most scientifically provable result of orgasm denial is an increase in testosterone. In the 1950s, Alfred Kinsey, the first scientist to study human sexuality in detail, described the orgasm as "an explosive discharge of neuromuscular tension."

The male orgasm is a complex system involving multiple hormones, organs, and nerve pathways. The hormone testosterone, which is produced in the testicles, plays a central role by enhancing the sexual desire libido that leads to arousal, erection, and ultimately orgasm. By contrast, low testosterone not only decreases a man's energy and mood, it makes him less responsive to sexual stimuli, both physical and mental. A man often only requires physical stimulation to achieve arousal, while women typically need physical and mental stimulation to achieve the same. Men differ from women in that their orgasms, the climax of the sexual response, come on faster and are shorter than women.

Ejaculation is a complicated process. According to Healthline, here's a quick breakdown:

1. The physical stimulation of sexual contact sends signals through the central nervous system to the spinal cord and brain.

2. This stimulation continues until you reach the plateau phase in the sexual cycle, which leads up to orgasm.

3. Tubes in the testicles that store and move sperm (the vas deferens) squeeze sperm out of the testicles into the urethra at the bottom of the penis.

4. The prostate gland and seminal vesicles produce fluid that will carry the sperm out of the shaft as semen. This then gets rapidly ejaculated out of the penis.

5. Muscles near the bottom of the penis continue to squeeze the penis tissues another five times or so to keep pushing semen out.

The refractory period happens right after you orgasm. It lasts until you're able to get sexually aroused again. The refractory period varies from person to person. A variety of factors affect it, such as your age and overall health.

As you age, it may take longer to get aroused and ejaculate. It may take between 12 to 24 hours between arousal and ejaculation. This timing differs for everyone. Studies show sexual function changes most drastically around 40 years old.

No Ejaculation and Increased Testosterone

Research on the relationship between ejaculation and serum testosterone levels in men who masturbated every day for a week, determined that when men don't masturbate for seven days, their testosterone levels increase by a whopping 45.7 percent. The significant testosterone increase could explain the purported physical benefits listed above and others, including a deeper voice, thicker hair, weight loss, greater strength, and power. It may also explain some of the psychological benefits, including increased energy and focus, increased courage, self-confidence, and by correlation, the testosterone boost could even be the reason that men perceived themselves to be more attractive to women when they did not orgasm.

Frequent Masturbation Decreases Androgen Receptors

But testosterone requires androgen receptors. Androgen receptors allow your body to use testosterone, such as to develop a deep voice and other manly traits. Without androgen receptors, testosterone is useless. Frequent masturbation hasn't been completely proven yet to really affect testosterone levels, however, overly active sexual activity like frequent masturbation has been proven, at least in lab mice, to significantly reduce the amount of androgen receptors in the body. It also boosts estrogen receptors, and it takes at least 15 days of abstinence to reverse these brain changes.

If a man constantly masturbates or orgasms, two events happen simultaneously. Dopamine plummets and prolactin soars. Dopamine is "go for the pussy!" and prolactin is "take a break!" This mechanism shifts a man's attention from sex to hunting and gathering, taking care of babies, building shelters, and so forth. Without this natural shutdown, men would, and god help us, pursue sex to the exclusion of all other activities 24/7.

In the study, androgen receptors participate in the neuroendocrine regulation of male sexual behavior, primarily in brain areas located in the limbic system. It regulates the relationship between sexual satiety and motivation, brain androgen receptors. And testosterone in men creates a long-term inhibition of sexual behavior after several ejaculations, known as sexual satiety. It has been shown that androgen receptor expression is reduced after a single ejaculation, whether during sex or masturbating. The study also found that the relationship between increased orgasming, which leads to a decrease in androgen receptors in specific brain areas and reduced sexual motivation independently of testosterone levels.

Dopamine is at the core of our sexual drives and survival needs, and it motivates us to do just about everything. This mechanism within the reward center of the primitive brain has been around for millions of years and has not changed. Rats, humans, and indeed all mammals share this common mechanism for survival. Dopamine is behind a lot of the desire we associate with eating and sexual intercourse. Similarly, all addictive drugs trigger dopamine and stimulate the pleasure/reward center. So do gambling, shopping, overeating, and other seemingly unrelated, activities. Go shopping—dopamine. Smoke a cigarette—dopamine.

Computer games—dopamine. Heroin—dopamine. Orgasm—dopamine.

They all work somewhat differently on the brain, but all raise your dopamine levels. You get a bigger blast of dopamine eating high-calorie, high-fat foods than eating low-calorie vegetables. You don't really love pizza, cheeseburgers, or ice cream sundaes, rather you really love that blast of dopamine that comes from it. You're genetically programmed to seek out high-calorie foods over others. Similarly, dopamine drives you to have sex over most other activities. With dopamine as the driving force, nature has designed your biology to engage in sex (fertilization behavior to make more babies). Dopamine also urges men to move on to new partners to create greater genetic variety among your offspring.

The primitive male brain accomplishes these goals of more offspring and promiscuity by manipulating a man's brain chemistry, and thus his desires and thoughts. High levels of dopamine increase a man's sexual desire, encouraging him to behave recklessly. It creates the thrill of a new affair and the rush from pornography. Unfortunately, consistently high levels of dopamine lead to erratic behavior and compulsions that are not good for a man's survival. That's why most mammals evolved with defined sexual periods when they "go into heat." The rest of the time they are more or less neutral about sex.

Humans, however, don't have a period of "heat" followed by a long period of indifference to sex. Unlike other mammals, humans have the potential for on-going, dopamine-driven sexual desire. Yet men self-regulate with an "off switch" that kicks in after they have too many orgasms. This drop in dopamine and rise in prolactin is the cause of the emotional separation that so often follows in the hours and even days after a man has sex and orgasms in a woman.

A balanced level of dopamine is necessary for good male mental health. When dopamine drops, men feel like something is wrong. Too much dopamine also leads to reckless behavior, which can be dangerous. Men then project these uncomfortable feelings onto their female partner. Wow, a sexual hangover! Suddenly, she doesn't look so appealing. This is a very uncomfortable cycle to experience in your ongoing Female Led Relationship and damages a couple's intimacy.

During this sexual hangover (low dopamine) period in the relationship, a woman may feel abandoned, and the man may feel like his woman is demanding sexual performance from him in a way that he simply cannot tolerate. This causes men and even women to desperately seek new highs like alcohol, sweets, new partners, pornography, and drugs. It is all just an effort to raise your dopamine levels after the fall.

Perhaps men can now see how this cycle of highs and lows, or attraction and repulsion, can make their Female Led Relationship feel more like a roller coaster ride than the romantic fairytale I promised in *Love & Obey*. It is like starting to drive and then slamming on the brakes in heavy traffic, and it can make your FLR sick. It shows up in lovers' lives as intense attraction, followed by boredom and even disgust. Prolactin promotes a desire for separation from your partner as well. What's worse is that dopamine is not the only culprit contributing to the behaviors and mood swings that separate intimate partners emotionally.

Prolactin, the neurochemical that shoots up after orgasm, is associated with many of the biggest complaints that long-term couples (female led and even male led) experience in their relationships. Prolactin's effects can linger. If you ever tried cocaine, you will know what I mean. Cocaine blasts the brain with high levels of dopamine and makes you feel incredible, but during cocaine withdrawal, prolactin rises and brings you way down, so you want more cocaine. Indeed, addicts going through cocaine withdrawal require two weeks for their prolactin levels to drop to normal and dopamine levels to rise.

After mating, female rats show surges in prolactin for a week or two, even if they don't get pregnant. Prolactin is associated with stress because it makes you feel like life is hopeless. As men grow distressed and discouraged by the puzzling highs and lows in their relationships caused by their orgasms and changes in dopamine levels, their higher prolactin levels only compound their distress and relationship unhappiness. They forget what it feels like to be in balance, and gradually lose their natural sense of wellbeing.

Both low dopamine and high prolactin levels make your world look dreary and increase your craving for more and better sex with new partners because your body naturally knows it will raise your dopamine levels. But, men, now you know that it will only set you on another sexually addictive cycle of highs and lows. Together, these neurochemicals create whatever couple knows as the "end of the honeymoon." Most male led couples experience this fatigue within the first year of marriage.

CHAPTER 5

The History of Orgasm Control

The history of chastity is unclear because most of the early versions were focused on women. The idea of the chastity device seems to have become popular in the 16th-century Renaissance when asking a woman to wear a chastity belt was a poet's way of saying, "Let us be true to each other." The first real chastity belts weren't created until the 1800s, and they were claimed to keep women from straying sexually. There may have also been another version of chastity belt as women began to enter the workforce during the dawn of the Industrial Revolution in the 1800s.

Most male chastity devices were born out of the need to control masturbation. Hartford, Connecticut, resident Daniel P. Cook in 1870 was one of the first to patent his male device, which he called the "self-protector." Ellen E. Perkins, also a pioneer of male chastity devices, of Beaver Bay, Minnesota, in 1907, said, "It is a deplorable but well-known fact that one of the most common causes of insanity, imbecility and feeble mindedness, especially in youth, is due to masturbation or self-abuse." So she created a device for the penis. Henry Tunnessen of Hazleton, Pennsylvania, who secured his patent in 1909 and said, "My object is to provide a device adapted to engage parts of the person and awaken the person in case of an erection of the parts so engaged, and thereby prevent involuntary nocturnal emissions."

Frequent masturbation was thought to shrink the penis and testicles, decrease the quality of the sperm, and even cause infertility. Nocturnal emission—releasing semen while you sleep due to erotic dreams or friction from your blankets—was believed to be the primary symptom of a fatal disease called "spermatorrhea" which was later found to not exist. The Jugnum Penis, also known as the Spermatorrhea Ring, was primarily designed to prevent wet dreams and nocturnal emissions. It consisted of a single spiked ring placed around the base of the cock just above the balls. Modern scholars and sexual historians have described it as something like a bear trap.

If the man developed an erection during the night, the spikes would dig into his penis, causing him to wake up to calm him down. Most barbaric of all were the anti-masturbation devices that could lead to permanent pain, scarring, or disfigurement. Some of these resembled old suits of armor and completely covered the cock, almost certainly leading to infection or disease since it could no longer be cleaned properly.

Others delivered electric shocks, ranging from mildly irritating to downright debilitating. Raphael Sohn patented the "Mechanical Sheath," a solid metal contraption locked by a key about the size of a fingernail. The Sheath resembled a modern cock cage—but much tighter. It was designed to squeeze the penis in a vice grip, preventing even the slightest motion. And should the wearer attempt to remove the cage without using their key, then it would cause the outer layers of the penis to be scraped and probably bleed.

There are many traditions and cultures that support orgasm control and many date back thousands of years. In Taoist sexual practices and traditional Chinese Medicine, there are three vital forces of life. Jing is the life force. It nourishes, fuels, and cools the body, and is an important concept in martial arts. One is said to be born with a fixed amount of jīng, but others believe you can acquire jīng from food and exercise, study and meditation. Jīng is therefore considered quite valuable for longevity. Jīng's most concentrated form is believed to be in semen, therefore sperm ejaculation is a direct and instant loss of jīng. This is where the power of semen retention originates.

In sexual intercourse with a woman, this powerful "jīng" life force energy is used to create a baby—new life—however, when "jīng" is lost during pulling out or masturbation, then that life energy is simply wasted. The production of semen in men, and menstrual blood in women, is considered to be the biggest strain on human's maintaining their jīng or life force. Many Taoist practitioners link the loss of ejaculatory "Jing" fluids to the loss of vital life force in which excessive fluid loss can cause premature aging, disease, and general fatigue. The general idea is that it is good for a man to limit his loss of semen as much as possible and to only allow male orgasm once in a great while. There's an old Taoist belief that controlling how often you ejaculate helps you preserve what's believed to be a finite amount of energy. Abstaining from ejaculation is thought to allow the energy contained in sperm and supply it with energy.

This practice is the origin of the "24 times a year" idea. In fact, some Taoist teachers recommend that you only ejaculate 20 to 30 percent of the times you have sex. That translates to two or three times out of every ten sessions. Another important concept of the Joining of the Male and Female Essence is that the union of a man and a woman will result in the creation of more jīng—sexual energy. If in the act of lovemaking, the man retains his jīng and transforms his life force and sex energy into a purposeful pleasuring and orgasming of the female, a man would see many health benefits in the long run. Hence the idea of fully satisfying the Queen's needs first.

In Hinduism, there are similar beliefs about semen retention. Shakti, or loosely translated to semen in English, also means power, ability, strength, might, effort, energy, capability. It is believed to be the primordial cosmic energy and represents the dynamic forces that are thought to move through the entire universe. Hindus believe that Shakti is both responsible for creation and the agent of all change. The most significant form of Shakti is thought to be the Kundalini Shakti, a mysterious psychospiritual force, which is said to be located at the base of the spine, equating with intense form of creative and sexual energy.

Today, chastity devices are evolving as we speak. Tech companies are designing app enabled locks, which most recently was hijacked by hackers, leaving many men powerless and trapped, probably having to go to the hospital. There are so many brand types and designs to choose from. But what has not changed is that the chastity device, to be effective in a relationship, must be used as part of a loving relationship controlled by the Queen.

CHAPTER **6**

Why Do Men Love Male Chastity?

Why do men love male chastity? Why would he welcome having his penis locked up and engaged in male chastity? The answer may not be apparent at first. To most people who are new to Female Led Relationships or domination and submission, they may fail to understand the inner workings of chastity, and they may find this practice to be abusive, barbaric, and downright inhumane. But just as all other practices which involve self-control and refraining from indulging in things, male chastity can lead to some very impressive and transformative results. As you have seen, at the physiological level, there are so many changes that occur.

If you ever had to go on a diet or give up drinking alcohol, the first few weeks were hell, but what happened long term? In terms of food, you lost weight and felt better, and in terms of alcohol, you felt clearer and also healthier. Male chastity is similar. In many cultures, we have seen that the constant indulging in masturbation and ejaculation leads to depletion of life force. It's similar to fasting. Many cultures believe in a period of refraining from indulgence as a means of strengthening the body.

We have also seen how male chastity conducted in a loving relationship, controlled by the woman, is transformative to men who later admit to becoming obsessed. Physically, a man feels better because his body is stronger and more energetic, he builds willpower and even more desire for his woman. He can focus all of his attention on his Queen, which is really what he wanted all along.

What happens to men and women in male chastity is similar to what happens during dating. The man is fixated on the woman, and desires sex with her, but the longer the fixation, the greater the desire. When you were dating, think of how many times you checked your phone, felt the excitement of seeing your man, and experienced little moments like the first kiss, holding hands, and the anticipation of sex. He was also 100 percent focused on you and your needs. and these are just some examples that make dating so exciting.

Once you are in a marriage or relationship for years, there is no pursuit and less desire and pretty soon, both of you are treating each other like an old shoe. You love your old shoe, and you would even be upset if you couldn't find your old shoe or it somehow disappeared, but it lost its novelty appeal. The anticipation, waiting, and desire for sex and togetherness is exactly what happens in male chastity when the Queen dictates when he should orgasm. Male chastity makes things new again because the woman now controls the power center of a man.

One of the fundamental aspects of social interaction is that some individuals have more influence than others. Social Power can be defined as the ability of a person to create conformity even when the people being influenced may attempt to resist those changes. Bosses have power over their workers, parents have power over their children, and, more generally, we can say that those in authority have power over their subordinates. In short, power refers to the process of social influence itself—those who have power are those who are most able to influence others.

Same is true when a woman has power over her man in the relationship or marriage. Men want a strong female figure in their lives so the idea of giving up the control and allowing their power centers to be controlled by a woman is very arousing. Once the Queen steps into her role as ultimate ruler and leader, the man will naturally take his position as the supporter. Ever need a man to make a grocery list on his own, then go get the groceries? He hates it. He is not interested in a leadership position in the household. Determine what he should get, give him a list, and he will gladly go do it. This is the supportive role and this is the role that men would prefer to be in.   Male chastity just takes being in the supportive submissive role to a whole new level. All of a sudden, men view their Queens in a much different light, which is why they get instantly aroused when the Queen places all of her attention on him and locks up his cock and holds the key. It's a symbol of ultimate control. Men also feel more testosterone, become stronger, more invigorated, and excited. His focus will naturally be on his Queen, and wearing the cage reminds him of whom he owes his allegiance.

In previous books, I have discussed the idea that men always need and respond to a leader. Without proper leadership, they feel chaotic with no direction and purpose. In the study *Sex-Role Obedience to Authority* by Geffner and Gross, obedience by male and female subjects to male and female experimenters was investigated. The four main factorial independent variables were the sex of the experimenter, the sex of the subject, and two conditions of presence or absence of a uniform presence or absence of an explanation. The results revealed there was more obedience with a uniform and more disobedience by females, which suggests that men are more likely to obey an authority figure.

Men need a purpose and a goal, so male chastity helps them to focus that purpose where it should be in all relationships— on the Queen.

Think about it—are you happier in a good, fulfilling deep relationship or a bad relationship with arguments and daily power struggle? With male chastity, there is no argument and men can do what they do best—be the supportive gentleman. This goes to the foundation of the female led lifestyle, which is why Female Led Relationships are so successful. Men love male chastity because each day is new and unpredictable and his Queen is focused on sex each and every day. When you are controlling his penis, you are in ultimate control over everyone else in his life. When he wears a cock cage, he will be thinking of you, all day long.

Going back to the research on men and authority—men respond much better when there is a firm authority figure in their lives. When they are younger, this person is their mother, and maybe their father. For at least 50 percent of the men out there, with divorce at 50 percent, men live and answer to a female figure, and it is believed that they crave this in a partner. The Queen replaces the mother as the authority figure, which is why Female Led Relationships are in demand. It's a win-win situation for you and your man because he will respond to your instruction, and you can be in charge.

CHAPTER 7

Why Do Women Like Male Chastity?

W omen love male chastity because there is no greater sign of devotion as when a man hands over the control of his most precious power. When you place a cage on his penis you signify that you essentially own him 100 percent. Male chastity really can only work when the relationship is loving and strong which is why a Female Led Relationship provides the perfect foundation.

Women are finally given the opportunity to be in complete control and have a man who dutifully serves her. This is a gift because we only become better versions of ourselves when we have the support we need to grow and evolve. Your man in a supportive position offers the Queen the support she needs to do what she does best—lead the relationship. The idea that you can now take it a step further and control your man's penis is only a bonus, but it represents a very powerful step. The first thing that happens is that every day, he is in chastity, and you, the Queen, put him in it, ramps up the sexual focus and it can make this process extremely exciting. When the Queen is turned on and eager to serve, this is likely to take intimacy and connectedness to a whole new level.

When a man gives up his "right" to ejaculate without his woman's permission and her allowing him to have intercourse with her, you are both stepping away from an old patriarchal conception of sex being performed for man's pleasure and that the man is independent, even when in a relationship form his woman's control. Once your man accepts male chastity, he is accepting a new sexual role. A role in which, you as the woman are in control, and he, as the man submits and can relax because he does not have to pretend that he is in charge anymore.

As your Female Led Relationship evolves, ejaculation itself may be separated from the couple's increasingly female focused sexuality. A man's "need" to ejaculate is vastly overrated and a clever wife can often train her husband to come on command, once a week or month, under her supervision. The rest of the time, if she desires, his oral attentions and, if she enjoys penetration, his hard but obedient penis are all that are required and he will become your obedient sex slave. Once a man realizes that he is no longer in charge of sexuality in your Female Led Relationship.

Once a man realizes that he is no longer even in charge of his own ejaculations, he may be confused about his role but trust me he will also be relieved of performance anxiety.

Male chastity will also help him retain his semen and raise his testosterone levels and sexual energy, so even his performance will improve, and he will more than likely be very hard and more than eager to perform for his woman when she wants to fuck him. This all helps to create the female's lead role as the man becomes the subject of her attentions, and enters the sub-zone where he is no longer obligated to initiate sex. In his new role, he will focus on how best to please his wife without thinking about his own pleasure because he knows that he will be aware that he is not going to be allowed to orgasm while pleasuring his wife—except on rare occasions when she allows him his special treat.

While men may find this is frustrating at first, most men are simple creatures and will soon accept their wife's complete control of the couple's sexuality. Better still, because the now dominant wife only has sex when she wants it and how she wants it. As a result, the couple will tend to be a lot more sexually satisfied. The man will quickly learn that he is now in the role of serving his woman's desires, not his own.

Men, on average, take four minutes from the point of entry until ejaculation. Women usually take around ten to eleven minutes to reach orgasm. This means there is a real need for men to slow down and for women to control their ability to orgasm in favor of their man focusing on their pleasure. Men and women travel slightly different paths to arrive at sexual desire. Esther Perel, a New York City psychotherapist, says, "I hear women say in my office that desire originates much more between the ears than between the legs. "For women, there is a need for a plot—hence the romance novel. It is more about the anticipation, how you get there; it is the longing that is the fuel for desire.

Women's desire "is more contextual, more subjective, more layered on a lattice of emotion," Perel adds. Men, by contrast, don't need to have nearly as much imagination, Perel says, since sex is simpler and more straightforward for them. That doesn't mean men don't seek intimacy, love, and connection in a relationship, just as women do. They just view the role of sex differently. "Women want to talk first, connect first, then have sex," Perel explains. "For men, sex is the connection. Sex is the language men use to express their tender loving vulnerable side," Perel says. "It is their language of intimacy."

Male chastity allows women to control the narrative and the lead up to sex. By controlling their man's ability to orgasm and keep the focus on them, they can create many different ways to engage in romance, foreplay, and sex. It allows women to shape sex to suit their needs, and this makes it more exciting for both. If the Queen is turned on, then her man is equally, if not more, motivated.

With female leadership in a relationship, the benefits don't stop at the bedroom door, a man who becomes sexually submissive to his woman will find that his own sexuality and sense of his masculinity will be transformed. He will become calmer and more at peace with himself. He will not have to be burdened with society's role of high sexual male expectations. He simply needs to do as he is told, and both he and his women will be happier than they ever imagined possible. Male chastity will make men better lovers. Once a man orgasms, the sex is usually done. By the woman not allowing or delaying the male orgasm, she essentially trains him to focus on her pleasure longer. You, the Queen, can spend more time enjoying multiple orgasms.

One of the most desirable benefits of male chastity happens shortly after the lock is shut for the first time. Once your man gets his first restricted erection after being locked, sexual tension and frustration will rise up, and your sub-male will have a powerful desire to channel it somehow. Naturally, his thoughts will move toward his Key Holder. This growing sexual frustration will build and the sub-male will find his Key Holder beyond irresistible. As the Key Holder, you will start receiving more frequent compliments, more affection and love, and your sub-male will become more romantic. And he will have so much more gratitude when you interact with him in any way, especially sexually, even if it is only for your pleasure like oral sex for you. Male Chastity quickly creates your dream partner!

Another noticeable benefit is the higher couple's sex drive that naturally comes as a result of the greater intimacy. As the pent-up male frustration and tension continues to build, the more his behavior will be toward making you happy. Soon both of your positive feelings toward each other will begin to overflow and the sex drive and libido will consume you both. Your man will want to pleasure you, the Key Holder as you have propelled into the number one spot in their mind.

Now instead of focusing on his own orgasm and masturbation, he is focused on everything he has to do to please his Queen. This is what every woman wants. It's the dream. The longer your man is locked, the more you will shape his behavior and the better he will become at serving you. When you demand oral sex to satisfy your needs first, the more practice he will get and the better he will be. All of a sudden, the bedroom will become so much more exciting and fulfilling.

Think of it as a female sexual guarantee that helps ensure your complete sexual satisfaction. Many men experienced premature ejaculation, and male chastity and orgasm control can train him to control his release. The Men's Clinic of UCLA says delayed ejaculation is the inability of a man to achieve climax within a reasonable amount of time. Some men cannot achieve ejaculation through vaginal penetration and must rely on alternative sexual acts to climax. Some men will lose their erection prior to achieving climax and be left frustrated. Some men will reach the point of orgasm but just can't finish and are left feeling very uncomfortable.

Delayed ejaculation is a neurological, hormonal, and psychological event. If a man has had damage to the nerves in his pelvis or had a spinal cord injury below the lower thoracic spinal level, he may suffer from inability to ejaculate. He lacks the nerve connection from the ejaculation nerves at the tip of his penis back to his spinal cord. More commonly, he may have a hormonal imbalance in serotonin, prolactin, or testosterone. Men taking antidepressants, whose serotonin levels are skewed by the pills, frequently suffer from delayed or loss of ejaculation. Men with low testosterone also can have difficulty ejaculating.

So if your man suffers from any of these conditions chastity can divert his attention from the sex act to pleasuring the

Queen or becoming aroused in other ways. Many men have reported feeling very aroused and fulfilled at the thought of just being under the Queen's control. Rather than place more stress on your man, male chastity allows him to relax and still enjoy sexual arousal and other forms of pleasure.

Lastly, masturbation can be a huge challenge for women. Many women are unhappy with the time their men spend masturbating. Men want sex more often than women at the start of a relationship, in the middle of it, and after many years of it. Men also say they want more sex partners in their lifetime and are more interested in casual sex. Men are more likely to seek sex even when it's frowned upon or even outlawed. About two-thirds say they masturbate, even though about half also say they feel guilty about it. By contrast, about 40 percent of women say they masturbate, and the frequency of masturbation is smaller among women.

The main purpose for sexuality is a union between two people who generally have some love and attraction for each other. The purpose of sexuality is abandoned in masturbation because the center of the sexual act becomes "me" instead of "we," and the person is trained to look to himself for sexual fulfillment. The gift of sexuality is misused for the sake of lifeless pleasure. When people misuse their sexuality in this way, they may begin to use pleasure to change their mood, release tension, or forget their loneliness.

Masturbation becomes an escape. It may pacify them, but it will never satisfy them. They use the fantasies of their mind and the pleasures of their body to flee from reality and the call to love. Their goal in sexual activity has been reduced to merely receiving pleasure instead of showing love. Women like chastity as a method to control their men masturbating. Chastity allows the Queen to control her man and the time he spends masturbating. In male chastity, a man's sexual energy should be reserved and focused on his woman.

CHAPTER 8

What is the Love & Obey Male Chastity?

The intent behind the Love & Obey Male Chastity and Orgasm Control Method of male chastity is to deepen the sexual and emotional connection and teach men to focus on their woman and not just their own needs. It's all about retraining men on how to properly worship you. Love & Obey and Female Led Relationships have always been about the loving worship of the Queen while following her lead. In male chastity, Love & Obey Male Chastity method means not only orgasm control or wearing a chastity device but now focusing your man's attention on you, the Queen, satisfying your needs first.

The traditional methods of male chastity really help to establish the authority and control of the Queen and helps your man to exercise self-restraint, self-control, and willpower. But now, Love & Obey takes it a step further by giving the man a purpose of having to pleasure the Queen as much as he can, while also learning willpower and abstinence.

One of the main purposes of the Love & Obey Male Chastity and Orgasm Control Method is to explore other forms of pleasure and train the man to focus on the female's pleasure above all else. *The Journal of Sex and Marital Therapy* in 2017 found that 37 percent of American women required clitoral stimulation to experience orgasm, compared to the 18 percent of women who said that vaginal penetration alone was sufficient to come. The focus for traditional love-making has always been on the man's orgasm, and the woman's is secondary, leaving many women unsatisfied. Female Led Relationships flip this and makes the woman's pleasure the first priority.

When you shift the experience and remove the focus from the male orgasm, this allows the man to focus on the woman and for you both as a couple to experience other sensations and a deeper connection. For men who tend to feel anxious during sex, which is often tied to feelings of inadequacy surrounding sexual performance and size, turning away from their own penis and orgasm and instead focusing on pleasuring the woman can alleviate this pressure.

In my opinion, a woman should never be reaching for her vibrator during sex with a man. A study shows that 63 percent of Millennials, 69 percent of Gen X'ers, and 75 percent of Boomers who are women are unsatisfied during sex. A man never has to reach for a tool to help him to orgasm, so why has this become an acceptable practice? If men practice the techniques in my book *Oral Sex for Women*, pleasuring the Queen should be possible.

When sex becomes about the journey for the man and not the destination, space is given to really enjoy each feminine sensation for what it is without becoming anxious about where it is leading for the man. His whole consciousness is on the woman's pleasure. We learn through male chastity that the orgasm is not the goal for everyone.

Sex therapist Jacqueline Mendez says, "What we're really looking for is connection. We want our partners to see us. We want to feel our partner's energy. We want to connect. It isn't always just sexual. It isn't always intercourse. It has to do with touch, feeling loved, acts of kindness. The more we're willing to see beyond the orgasm, we begin to notice sexual satisfaction begins in other realms of daily life. Foreplay begins the moment we open our eyes. Men can participate by engaging their partners, paying attention to the nuances of the day, paying attention to personality, wants, needs so that when they do get to that space of having sexual activity, it can be a physical manifestation of loving they've had all day."

The Love & Obey method of Male Chastity and Orgasm Control encourages couples to take their time caressing, touching, kissing, and snuggling with each other. These actions stimulate the production of oxytocin, a neurotransmitter that promotes feelings of bonding and love. Caressing for longer and longer periods of time makes us feel good, happy, and pain-free. In the case of a Love and Obey Female Led Relationship, when we make love-making about worshipping the Queen and prolonging this experience, it can make the overall session so much more powerful and enjoyable.

A husband practicing male chastity is made attentive, romantic, and obedient because of his Queen who is in charge. She is happier because her husband will do anything to satisfy her needs. Sometimes we are so overwhelmed by life and responsibilities that in life we barely notice there is a lack of connection. This does not happen in a proper Female Led Relationship because the focus of the Queen is to lead each and every day, and the man must devote his time to making his woman happy. It's a win-win situation, and it solves a number of problems which can lead to the destruction of the relationship.

But with male chastity, there is a desperate need for the locked male to be completely in touch with his Key Holder or experiencing the same frequency. This union is inherently harmonious, and when harmony is experienced in sex, it will usually find its way outside of the bedroom. In other words, the time spent on connecting during sex for a couple living in a Love & Obey Male Chastity and Orgasm Denial inclusive relationship will help to strengthen the relationship as a whole.

Love & Obey Male Chastity and Orgasm Control is at its core a spiritual practice. The focus is on bringing these two powerful forces together to worship the female and serve her on a higher level. If penetrative sex isn't an option for some due to a disability or a condition like erectile dysfunction, the Love & Obey Male Chastity and Orgasm Denial method offers another way to enjoy sexuality with a partner that almost anyone can enjoy because it allows you to focus on caressing, embracing, and oral sex rather than penetration.

The focus on the spiritual side is important. In the movie *The Upside* with Kevin Hart in the role of Dell Scott, I was struck at how his physically disabled boss, Phillip Lacasse, was able to be sufficiently turned on simply by having his ears massaged. As the leader of the Love & Obey Female Led Lifestyle movement and having communicated with thousands of couples worldwide, I have come to see firsthand how orgasm control transforms relationships.

Countless women have used this method to help their men with premature ejaculation issues or erectile dysfunction. Men all over the world have admitted they enjoyed the process of discovering more excitement with their current partner, and they had less desire for masturbation, porn, or outside sexual encounters. Orgasm control takes time and practice for men. It requires setting of mini-milestones as they experiment with it and get better and better at controlling their orgasms. The results are beneficial for men, as they become far more powerful lovers than previously.

Adding male chastity into your relationship will create a renewed dating experience. When considering male chastity, the first thing we need to look at is how men think and act. Understanding basic male behavior is so important to a woman who is interested in building a Female Led Relationship and taking charge of her man. Think back to when you and your partner started dating. Remember how attentive, considerate, and caring he was to you on those first dates. Remember how he did those "little things" for you to show you how special you were to him. Remember how romantic he was during that "courting period" and how he went out of his way to make sure that you got whatever you wanted.

He was focused on satisfying all of your needs so he could get in your panties. He also showed some consideration when he finally got sex and made sure that you got pleasure and satisfaction out of having sex with him. Contrast that to later when he is just thinking about his pleasure and not worrying about whether you even orgasm or not. Ladies, those days are gone, between Female Led Relationships and Male Chastity, men now will be trained to perform for you, and orgasm you first or they won't get our incredible gifts again.

Unfortunately, men become comfortable in long-term relationships, especially in male led marriages after some time. Men become lazy and complacent and stop thinking about your emotional, romantic, and sexual needs. Women have admitted to starting a Female Led Relationship so that the focus is back on them. Male chastity and orgasm control fixes selfish male behavior when the goal of sex is turned upside down. Now the goal of sex is not your man's ejaculation. It's first your orgasm and then if you decide he deserved to have his orgasm, only then is it about his pleasure after you have been fully satisfied.

As we have learned, orgasm control has so many benefits, including keeping the focus on you. Have you ever watched a cat that relentlessly pursues a bird or a mouse? It is obsessed with its prey. It cannot for one second stop pursuing it and it will chase almost continuously with the desire to catch it. But once the cat kills the mouse, it immediately loses interest. I would add that it is the obsessive desire to achieve the goal of catching, which controls and motivates the cat.

Humans also need a goal, and men are especially programmed to hunt. So, the desire is extinguished, as when he gets his sexual satisfaction, then he is ready to move onto the next exciting thing. Smart, powerful, influential women understand this and female led women know how to control it. This is the reason male chastity is so powerful and for women who understand how to use it means the ultimate control over your man. The Queen has the ultimate control, and he will be obsessed with trying to please you.

There is a big difference between the male chastity fantasy of being locked in a device for one sexy night and the actual reality of a woman not unlocking her man's penis from his cage unless he is 100 percent obedient to her every command. Once he realizes you, as his woman, have truly taken control of the key and of all of his future orgasms, then you have all the power. Once a woman is holding the key to the Male Chastity device, which is locked on your man's penis, all the cards are stacked in the female's favor, and the real sexual pleasure and benefits are reaped by the Key Holder—not the man.

That's why I love male chastity and encourage every woman to make it a central focus of her Female Led Marriage or Relationship. You'll be shocked at how often he begs to go down on you after he has been locked for a while. Once you experience the benefits, which can be achieved from very little effort by the Key Holder, you will wonder why you didn't get started with Male chastity and a "Cock Cage" on your man years ago! Believe me, you'll be glad once you do it and amazed at how wonderful your life will become because of Male Chastity.

Male chastity teaches a man respect and obedience to women. It is a physical tool to remind him that he is not in charge and \has no rights other than those given to him by his woman. Now he becomes grateful to his Key Holder for any pleasure given to him. He thanks her for letting him lick her. He thanks her for letting him penetrate her. It is a privilege that he receives from his woman. Not something that he can bully or force his way to take whenever he has the desire for sex. All men should approach older women respectfully as mother figures and all younger women who are not his loving female authority as his sisters.

When his woman uses familial terms to describe women to her man, she sets the rules for chaste conduct by men toward women. Over time this will have the mental conditioning ability to end abuse and rape by men. A woman's message should be clear: Every man should treat every woman respectfully, the way they would treat their own mother or sister. Only when his woman allows a man to be released from his cage, solely for female sexual worship, can he be allowed to think of a woman in sexual terms.

A man's loving female authority should teach him through male chastity to treat women as his superior and with respect. Men should always use respectful speech and conduct to show their Loveland devotion to their women when speaking to women in every other sector of life. This demonstrates living a loyal and devoted life to one Mistress, Queen, or Goddess. It stops masturbation to pornography, cheating with other women, and upholding a virtuous reputation of total devotion to his chosen female partner. In all ways, a man is only allowed to do what his female partner permits, and part of this must be to teach the man that he must learn to be respectful to all women, not just his female partner.

CHAPTER 9

Create an Amazing Male Chastity Experience?

How do you create an amazing male chastity experience, one that will be exciting, fulfilling, and pleasurable? The first thing you need to do is to create the rules, schedule, rewards, and overall process. The Queen needs to begin by creating the rules and both you and your man need to come to an agreement about what will happen. He should be reminded of proper ways to respond and what will be expected of him. Men respond to carefully laid out rules about conduct and wearing the device. Reinforce him daily about how happy you are that he is in male chastity and how excited you feel. Mention this later on in the day. You can give them explicit information on how and where, and when it's going to happen or tell him it will be a surprise. Get him excited and sexually frustrated. Let him think about the orgasm you may or may not let him have later.

As with everything in a Love & Obey relationship, communication is key. Communication is critical and putting your man in a male chastity device is no exception. Start by talking to your male partner about what it is that appeals to you about having him locked and you holding the key, and find out what might appeal to him about it. Not only should you talk about it before, but you'll want him to give you feedback once he is wearing his device. It's all part of his male submission to you, and it should never be taken for granted— make sure that he is happy with the planned pleasures of your new area of control over him.

Her Erogenous Zones

As part of male chastity, the man is required to serve the Queen in any way she desires. In a study, 91 percent of men reported that they usually always orgasm during sex, whereas only 39 percent of women reported they consistently come during sex. This has to change, and it means that if his penis is locked up, he is free to focus on any number of erogenous zones on her body and vice versa. In female led and male chastity, this has to change. The focus has to be on the Queen's orgasm and pleasure. Here are some areas to focus on:

1. Clitoral Stimulation

The first most obvious area for women is clitoral stimulation, which can be vital in achieving orgasm, as most people find those sensations are the easiest way to experience orgasm. Stimulate the clitoris with the fingers, tongue, or sex toys by gently rubbing in a circular motion. Make sure the clitoris is adequately lubricated as this will increase those tingly sensations.

2. G-spot

Often called the magic spot of female sexual pleasure, the G-spot is located about an inch inside the vaginal opening, on the vaginal wall closest to the belly button. Stimulating the G-spot can lead to powerful orgasms, and even female ejaculation. Combining clitoral stimulation with G-spot stimulation can result in a heavenly blended orgasm.

3. Nipples

Pinch, stroke, twist, lick, kiss, blow... Having someone play with your nipples can have an orgasmic effect. With concentrations of nerve endings and the possibility of nipple orgasm, nipples are a serious pleasure zone that is so often overlooked. Nipples are extremely responsive and can withstand stronger stimulation the more you get in the mood! However, everyone's sensitivity is different—some nipples are highly sensitive, whilst others can withstand a hard squeeze. Always start with light touches, and gradually build up the intensity and pressure. If you like a lot of stimulation, talk about investing in nipple clamps to teeter that line of pain and pleasure. As ever, it is important to communicate what you are comfortable with and what feels good.

4. Perineum

A well-known male erogenous zone but a lesser-known female hot spot. The little area of skin that sits between the vagina and anus. This area can be aroused through gentle massage or touching. Incorporate touching of this area when indulging in oral sex, with a gentle lick, you'll be surprised how good this feels.

5. Ears

As mentioned before, ears can be very sensitive, erogenous areas. Massaging the earlobes can often relax you, so why not try a gentle stroke, pull, or twist to deliver some extra endorphins. For something a little more sensual, a light lick, nibble, or suck can leave you in the mood with those tingly feelings.

6. Stomach

Sitting right about the vulva, this hot spot is often kissed and licked in the build-up to oral stimulation. Try some temperature play, which will leave you breathless with sexual tension in the air. Drip candle wax over the stomach or try rubbing an ice cube along the stomach and navel—the contrast between temperatures will awaken some delightful sensations. The area between the belly button and the pubic area can often trigger a pleasure response, which is another area that is often tied to oral sex. By stimulating this area with your hands or mouth, you can actually stimulate the G-spot from the opposite side.

7. Inner thighs

This erogenous zone is great for teasing within the build-up to oral stimulation just like the stomach. Gently kiss the inner thighs, tracing your tongue up to get closer and closer to the vagina. With consent, gentle bites can increase sexual arousal whilst sending you into the pleasure zone.

8. Lower back

Light touches and tickles along the small of your back can leave you feeling close to your partner through the sensual nature of the touches. This spot is perfect for a little sensory stimulation; try a feather or an ice cube for some delicious sensations.

9. Armpits

Armpits are really sensitive and ticklish as there are lots of nerve endings. It can be a very erogenous zone. Not everyone likes it, so should start slow and build up with touching.

10. Scalp

Scalp massages are wonderful, alongside the tingling and pleasurable sensation you feel as the technique also decreases stress and boosts your mood. The feeling of your man's hands on your head can be a real turn on for you and him.

11. Neck

By giving the neck some loving, the make-out session can become a more holistic experience. Gentle neck kisses and licking can be such a turn on due to the high concentration of light-touch receptors.

12. Fingers

Holding hands is very intimate alone, as it can make you feel connected to your partner. Or make this more sensual by sucking on someone's fingers. A light suckingcan produce a pleasurable feeling as the gentle waves of sensation.

13. Bum

Increase arousal with some kisses and squeezes. The bum can provide endless fun for teasing and pleasure. If full-on penetration scares you a little, then try some light touches and caressing of the outside skin. Remember, if you do want to amp things up further with some ass play, then use plenty of lube.

14. Mouth

Kissing is a powerful tool, and by paying some special attention to the mouth you can turn up the heat and intensity. Build intimacy and a deeper emotional connection to your partner through gentle kisses. Escalate this further by varying pressure and intensity to spark passionate feelings. Not only does giving special attention to the mouth feel incredible, but it is a vital part of foreplay.

15. Inner wrist

The ability to feel the pulse in this area means it is one of the most vulnerable intimate areas on your body. By lightly caressing and kissing, you will feel like your soul is bared to your partner.

16. Feet

Stimulate and pleasure feet with objects, such as a feather or just a light tickle. This area can be sexually arousing for some people, and if you want to delve into the world of foot foreplay, then have a look at our foot foreplay ideas.

17. Knee

This area is incredibly sensitive to touch, so focus on this spot during a massage building pressure. Careful, as this area can be incredibly ticklish for some.

Male chastity needs to be clearly defined as your man's time to pleasure and serve you first. You can also add some teasing, tempting, and additional play like spanking, bondage, blindfolding, and any other fun playful methods to increase excitement. The most important part of chastity is that you make it ceremonial. When you place the cage on your man, it should be followed by a period of. "Yes Goddess, I serve you and only you." Make it an important part of the day for both you and your man to refocus your attention.

Sometimes daily chores and activity can get in the way of the relationship, so make your act of putting on his cage and removing it special. Re-enforce all of the important parts of a Female Led Relationship and have him read my book *Oral Sex for Women* so that he can properly serve his Queen during the periods of chastity. Only by doing these practices daily will the principles of chastity be understood and experienced. It is possible to begin with just exploring orgasm control. Setting times when he can orgasm and when he cannot will help him get into the practice of complete abstinence, then he can proceed to use the cage during longer periods of chastity. It is best to use a schedule of build up for chastity so that he becomes comfortable and doesn't become overly stressful.

Here are some additional rules for her man to follow:

1. **The Queen, and only the Queen, is in charge.**

2. **You will wear the chastity device on command.**

    The Queen knows that she holds the power and her man will follow without argument.

3. **You shall provide sex upon command.**

    The submissive partner has to please their dominant at any given time of the day.

4. **Ask for permission before you cum.**

5. **Remember who you belong to.**

    You will have no other sexual partners but the Queen. By being monogamous, it lets her know that she is in full control. and she is the focus.

6. Make the Queen proud

Making the Queen master proud actually has a deeper meaning. It's not just about the pleasing of their physical needs but also about making them proud of you in every aspect of your life. This will improve both your physical and mental health because you will feel sensations of accomplishment, trust, and the ultimate bond.

7. I speak, you obey.

Whatever the Queen wants, she gets. Never interrupt her. Allow her to speak first, then you may respond. Arguing with the Queen is forbidden.

The reason male chastity transforms relationships is because when your man submits, it requires an extraordinary amount of trust, not to mention courage and confidence too. It immediately changes the dynamic. Accepting his devotion also comes with great responsibility, so the Queen must also step into the role of leadership, and she is expected to honor that trust. Once a man obeys the Queen, he needs to be rewarded. Even though male chastity involves you being in control, you must reward him for his good behavior. This can be with the promise of unlocking him so that he can have intercourse and orgasms, or you can do lots of teasing and reminding him of who is the ultimate woman in his life.

For him to remain motivated, you must keep the sexiness alive. Constant reminders of how he pleases you, teasing him, adding role play, wearing costumes, giving massages and touching can go a long way to keeping the excitement alive. Male chastity must be respected. Show him how proud you are of his efforts to show his devotion. Male chastity should never be used to abuse or neglect your man. It is the opposite. It requires daily attention and to focus on each other and reinforcement. Your man is doing something no other human being in the world will do for you and his sacrifice and devotion must be honored. Each day, as the Queen, you will determine the course of the interaction. He will be looking to you for leadership. So placing him in chastity is one step, but how you reward him is equally important. It is this exchange that makes male chastity so exciting and transformative.

CHAPTER 10

How to Perform Love & Obey Male Chastity

T he whole point of chastity is heightening the experience outside of the bedroom in daily life as well as inside of the bedroom. Since during sex is where most of the excitement will occur, it is beneficial to add some of these tips to your sex session. Sex should be made to be very special, even while using chastity, so I advise creating an intentional, sensual, intimate, romantic bedroom atmosphere. The entire session should be focused on pleasure and worship. Make the room warm and inviting by using some scented candles, satin sheets, sexy decorations, and lay out all of your toys, including your chastity cage.

Some couples like to make it very ceremonial in which the women put on her Queen's robe. Play some soft sexy music. Make sure you remove all distractions like phones and put the kids to bed. Before you begin, you may want to direct him to put on his chastity cage and model it for you. Then he begins by worshipping and kissing your feet or rubbing your shoulders. A full-body massage is always nice. He is showing his complete focus and devotion to you wearing his device and attending to getting you warmed up and calmed down. Perhaps you can order him to bring you your favorite glass of wine. You can begin by getting him comfortable attending to you.

Next, set intentions for the sexual session as a couple. You both should enter the sexual session with a specific mindset about what type of experience you're trying to create. Keep in mind that the practice is meant to be about touching and being in touch with the whole body. Maybe the intention is more connection. Maybe it's exploring how to increase just teasing or just foreplay. Maybe you both want to meditate together for a few minutes or clear the energy of any past arguments. The intention can be how aroused can he make you or just focusing on oral sex. This allows you to make every single sex session different.

Have you explored new areas of each other's bodies? Maybe you had no idea he was turned on by rubbing the bottom of his feet or he loved touching your lower back and inner thighs. This is your time to request and demand anything you want to try. It is important to re-enforce that his orgasm is second. He has to fully commit to making you extremely turned on and aroused before beginning to think of his own pleasure. You, as the Queen, will need to step up and give him direction. Maybe you want him to wear his cock cage the entire time, or you will want to remove it when you are now ready to receive his divine penis. You will need to instruct him.

Let him know to start slowly and sensually. Begin by massaging or gently running his fingertips over your goddess body. Have him pay attention to places he might normally neglect during sex. He will caress your face, neck, shoulders, and the sides of your waist. Place a heavy emphasis on communication and tell you how you are worshipped, his dedication to serving you and desire to give her as much pleasure as possible. He will ask what feels good and how the sensations feel on your body. As he touches you, tell him where he should linger with his touch, lips, and tongue. Be direct about what maximizes your pleasure.

Remind him that he must compliment you, and as he wears his chastity device for you as a sign of his devotion, have him explain why he adores you and what he loves about you. Some couples find this to be humor, but it is an important and often overlooked part of the worship session. Some couples get a Queen's throne, and he must kneel before the Queen and tell you how beautiful you are. Flattery will get him everywhere. You, in return, can tell him how much you adore his devotion or the way he serves you. The more you encourage his proper behavior and treatment of you, the more it spills over into daily life.

Sex in female led worship must be ceremonial. It breaks the boredom. The courtship and build up, as well as foreplay, is extremely important in long-term relationships. Let's face it, you've done everything after a while in relationships, but if you are new to chastity and Female Led Relationships, you will be new to many of the ways you can show your dominance and he shows his submission. Some women have their men dance like strippers. One woman put up a pole, and they took turns doing sexy dances. She said her husband was very uncoordinated, but he enjoyed trying to tease her. So have fun trying new things.

Use foreplay to do lots of fooling around with your husband, such engaging in your usual kissing, cuddling, and petting as you typically would do without the cage, but you can also show some attention to his cock cage, which makes things even hotter. Use your femininity to your advantage by dressing and undressing seductively to heighten the mood, and employ whatever little tricks you know are particularly effective at turning him on. The more you can seduce and tease him, the more the feeling of being restrained becomes electrifying. His penis may swell like it wants to break the cage, but the sense of restriction can be surprisingly erotic in itself, especially as he anticipates his release. As the Queen, you must demonstrate your control and power over him. You can say things like, "I am your ultimate supreme ruler. I own you, and you will always do as I command."

Tease him about how excited he's getting, telling him how much he must enjoy being kept under lock and key to have become so hard in his cage. It's perfectly natural for a man to become aroused under such circumstances, but that doesn't mean you can;t use this to your advantage by employing a little psychology to direct his thoughts in the direction you want them to take. As well as teasing him physically, you can verbally remind him of his plight, whispering sweet nothings in his ear about how much you're looking forward to having him pleasure you later.

By telling him of your own satisfaction, you help reinforce his understanding that your sexual needs must come before his own. Let him know how hot the thought of keeping him under lock and key is making you—something that will not only turn him on, but help overcome any reluctance on his part about wearing the device for you. Once you're sure he's all worked up, ask him how it feels to be entirely at your mercy or how much he wants to come—suggest impossible, ridiculous, or humiliating things you might have him do in order to be let out, all the better if he doesn't know whether to take you seriously or not.

Show off the key and that you alone hold the power to release him, pending his complete devotion to you. Not only does this serve to heighten his frustration, maximizing the sexual tension of the situation, he now understands he has no choice but to obey your wishes should he wish to be released from it.

When it's time to get close, make sure he caresses you all over and around your vagina, kissing you and warming you up before beginning oral sex. Refer to my book *Oral Sex for Women* if your man requires some brushing up of his technique. While he wears his cage, he must work toward giving you a mind-blowing oral sex session. You may decide to remove his cage before or after. You are free to explore what works better. When you feel ready to have intercourse, you can remove the cage as you possess the key.

You can make it very ceremonial—the Queen has decided to now remove your cage. Then once it's removed, you can begin intercourse, slowly where he is now using his devoted penis to pleasure you. Even as he thrusts, he should gauge how you are feeling. You must be vocal about how you feel. If you want him to kiss your neck or your breasts, order him to do it. The Queen must tell her man what she desires, and he must do it. Maybe you need him to go slower as he kisses you or go faster. You must be into it as much as he is. Direct him, give him feedback, and control the sex session. If he fails to sufficiently satisfy you, maybe his penis needs to go back into its cage. During sex, you have free reign as the Queen to decide how the session goes. Will you allow him to orgasm? If no, then he must not.

He is simply not allowed to come. If the Queen desires he has an orgasm, then you can direct him. Take it slow. Pleasuring you should never be like a marathon. Mix up oral pleasure with intercourse to practice feminine worship properly. Always be loving, kind, and patient with your man. Slow, gentle, and tender are desired by most women, so remember that on your female led journey.

Love & Obey Male Chastity and Orgasm Control takes male chastity to a whole new level, and it should be performed almost as a ritual. As the Queen, you may decide your man needs to show devotion first thing in the morning by greeting you as the Queen or when he comes home at night. You decide during sex how you want the session to run. Will he begin by giving you a full-body massage, kissing all of your erogenous zones, then orally pleasuring you all while he is wearing his penis cage? Maybe you want to add some spanking or bondage and engage in a bit of this play before moving on to oral pleasure. Or maybe you decide he will only pleasure you for the entire night, and he is not allowed to orgasm. There are so many ways in which you can add chastity, but what is important is that for the Love & Obey method, he is increasing your pleasure. The orgasm control serves to give him an opportunity to pleasure you first.

When you're satisfied, and he's made an appropriate effort, you should reward him. Take the opportunity to link his satisfaction with your own, toying with the lock on his chastity device as you ask him whether he deserves to be released. "Have you been a good boy?" "Shall I let that mighty monster of yours out of its cage now?" "Did you make me happy first?" Don't forget to reward him with praise for an outstanding performance. Unlock the cage in a mini-ritual as well. Have him ask or even beg to be released before you remove it. Let him know the Queen has decided to let him out. Then make him kneel before you, kiss your feet, or show his gratitude. Mix it up and have fun.

After the initial introduction to male chastity, you can evolve to have him wearing it for longer periods of time. On a night out, you can have him wear it as you tease him, kiss him, touch him all through the night. The feelings of intense pressure, plus your constant attention, will drive him wild. It could become so intense that he may want you to pull over and have sex. By having him keenly await your lovemaking, rather than simply taking it for granted, you encourage him to regard it as something special that should be enjoyed. After one night, he can progress to a full-day and daily life. Now you can take your dominance to a whole new level by ordering him to do tasks, chores, and anything else you need done—all under your control.

Remember, there are levels to chastity: light, medium, strict. Light involves the Queen's refusal of her man to cum. This can increase the intensity of the orgasm. Orgasm denial is a time-honored sexual amplifier. Done within the context of a committed relationship, it is an awesome way to start. Medium involves chastity without devices but is much more long-term. As the Queen, you decide your man cannot come for the day or two. Sex for several sessions is reserved for the Queen. The Queen can also request the pull out method or just have oral sex alone on those days. She may also demand that her man complete chores before he is allowed to cum.

The strict level is the use of the chastity device and or long-term chastity. At this level, the Queen demands her man wears the device and she holds the key, only allowing him out when she desires it. The Queen can also keep her man in chastity for longer periods or he wears his device at work. Some couples choose to create a contract in the strict version of male chastity. Both you and your man write down the rules in contract form, and you both sign it as your promise to adhere to it. Sometimes making a formal agreement helps you both to understand what is expected and sets intentions, boundaries, and commitment. There are so many options to explore. You can also begin at the light level and progress to stricter as you both become more serious. No matter what you choose, it must be a joint effort with consent from both of you. Male chastity is not fixed. There is ample room to explore, which creates so much opportunity to evolve.

CHAPTER 11

The Male Chastity Device

O ne million chastity devices were sold by one brand in the last 12 months, and it's sure to be a huge seller for the holidays. The most popular male chastity device is the chastity cage that is worn around the penis to restrict it. The main purpose of a male chastity device is to force your man to surrender control of his penis to you, the Queen, who holds the key. Most chastity devices are similar to handcuffs, so it is difficult to remove, and it fastens around a part of the body that's narrow. Once locked in place, such devices take advantage of the wearer's anatomy to keep them from falling off, in the same way that a handcuffed man cannot slip his bonds without them being loosened first.

There are three main types. Firstly, some cages and tubes make use of a cock ring behind the testicles to stay in place—ideal for beginners thanks to their price and convenience. More traditional chastity cages fasten around the waist or hips, offering greater security once the wearer has become accustomed to them, although more expensive. Finally, there are smaller tubes that employ a piercing through the penis to prevent them from being removed. The most popular is the first type—the chastity cage. Each type of male chastity device has its own advantages and disadvantages, but fundamentally work the same way, preventing the wearer from touching or stimulating his penis without the Key Holder's permission. The differences between the various kinds of device lie in comfort, cost, security, and convenience as the main factor when it comes to choosing the right one for you and your partner. There is no one choice that is best for everyone.

There are two main parts to putting on a cock cage. The first is putting on the ring. To do this, you should first put each testicle through one at a time. Then bend the penis downwards and slide it in as well. Once you've done this, you can place the enclosure of the cage over the penis and attach it to the ring. Some cages don't come in two completely separate parts, but instead have a hinge between the ring and the enclosure. If this is the case, you should insert the testicles the same way, then bend the penis upwards so the enclosure can hinge over it and into place or downwards, depending on where the hinge is.

Chastity devices do take some work. First, you must figure out how to put it on and take it off safely. It also has to be cleaned every day. Your man needs to be trimmed, so it doesn't pinch his hair. He will have to be cautious when using a restroom. For beginners, they may have difficulty standing and relieving themselves. Sitting may be better. This will take some practice, and each man has to develop this technique for himself. It will be a whole learning experience for most men, and how to deal with it in a practical way like learning how to sleep through the night. When your man tries it for the first time, he will need to get adjusted to it. Many men cannot sleep at night, because they get erections while they sleep or when they wake up in the morning. However, these devices are made so that men can't get an erection, so they wake up and have to figure out a way to get their penis to go down and then go from there. For many men, the answer is simple; if you just pee, your erection will go away.

Once your man puts on the chastity cage, there may be a few challenges. The first is there will be a feeling of extra weight and bulk on the penis. It pulls the penis downwards quite a lot and can be very irritating. The best way to deal with this is to wear tighter underwear, so the cage and penis are kept close to the body, and some of the weight is supported by the fabric. Another potential issue is chafing and skin irritation. The ring of the cage will naturally move around while he wears it, rubbing against the skin, and some people may experience rashes or rough areas of skin. This can be avoided by applying some lube around the ring at regular intervals, giving it the ability to move more freely without friction against your skin. If the ring is causing irritation, it's a good idea to use some moisturizing cream to help treat the area. Almost all cages can be cleaned with warm soapy water. Be sure to use a cloth and get into all the small crevasses, as these are the places bacteria are most likely to build up. All cock cages should be stored in a cool, dry place. Ideally, each should be in its own container or plastic bag, as this reduces the risk of cross-contamination.

When you are choosing the right device, be sure to review all reviews and read as much information as you can about the different brands. The last thing you need is to have bought and returned several devices. Choose brands that are of high quality. As with anything you put on your body, ensure you don't have any allergies or skin disorders that may be aggravated. Once you find the right one, you are ready to give it a try.

CHAPTER 12

How to Use the Chastity Cage

O ne of the first major steps to complete devotion is use of the chastity cage, and it is likely to create a major paradigm shift in the relationship. As we have learned, when a man is placed in chastity, he immediately refocuses his attention on the Queen. He will require almost 100 percent of your attention, and this is a good thing, because he is now firmly under the control. One of the first steps is to have a conversation about wearing the device. Both you and your man have to be in agreement. He in particular because he will have to endure some discomfort. Once you have established that it is something you both want to explore, you have to get on finding the right one. Some of these goals you may want to address with chastity are:

- How to get him to appreciate you more rather than merely taking things for granted.

- How to stop him from masturbating or being tempted by pornography behind your back.

- How to get him to pursue you the same way when you were first dating.

- How to encourage him to slow down and spend more time on your pleasure.

Be prepared for some opposition and growing pains. Men are not all dying to be locked up in a device and depending on where he is in his female led training, he may be against it completely. In addition, even if he welcomes chastity, he may feel frustrated with the whole idea, including finding the right device. So, spend some time discussing all of his concerns and explore as many different brands for the device as you can. The device should fit properly and securely. Male Chastity devices are an experience where you lock your man's penis in a specially designed cage that prevents him from getting full erections and using his penis for sexual purposes. While locked up, he can't engage in intercourse, masturbate, or orgasm, and the cage can only be removed by his designated female Key Holder.

What is the Significance of the Key Holder?

While the thought of giving ultimate control over to his goddess may make some men cringe, it can also make them excited. Being caged by his goddess can be extremely thrilling and fulfilling. The Key Holder is symbolic of the ultimate leader and woman in his life. For many men, this can be a moment of complete submission. Many women experience men having more allegiance to their mothers than their wives or girlfriends, but once he submits to you, you become his ultimate leader. His Queen as the Key Holder becomes the most important person in his life. In addition, as we have discussed, orgasm denial increases the man's sex drive and improves his focus on the female's needs and desires. It also obviously heightens the stakes of a Love & Obey Female Led Relationship, with a Queen able to punish her man by denying him not just sex but his ability to orgasm.

For men who have chosen a Female Led Relationship, it's the "not getting off" part that excites them, and it's the giving up something for your superior female. It is also for men who are into someone having a certain level of control over them. These are the men who like someone giving commands, such as saying "Wear this shirt," or "Massage my feet,"—the female control is what gets them excited. Male chastity is an extension of that. The man is giving up control of his beloved penis to his superior female. They are letting the female decide when he can have sex, orgasm, and be released from his cage. For many men, it's like wearing something sexy without people not knowing about it. It is really a low-level form of bondage that your man can wear every day.

Since the Queen makes the decisions on how long to wear the device and when to take it off, there are many ways in which she can place her man in chastity. You can have him wear a chastity device before you have sex so that he can only spend time providing oral satisfaction. You can also make wearing the chastity device foreplay. Have him wear it for an hour before engaging in sex. This gives him plenty of time to anticipate any action that may be forthcoming, allowing you to work his passions up into a frenzy should you so desire. As well as getting your husband all fired up, teasing him sexually during this time serves to strengthen this most intimate of bonds between you, and is all the more effective thanks to him being helpless to resist.

Spending a day at work locked in such a device is a great way of getting him in the mood for an evening in, providing a constant, unforgettable reminder of just what he's coming home to. It's a sexy secret you'll share however far apart you might be, even when he's in the most humdrum of meetings or up to his ears in paperwork. If you prefer, you can prolong his chastity further—a few days at a time works well as a means of making things up to you, or simply to get him all hot and bothered over the course of a weekend. You can progress to longer periods once he gets used to wearing it.

It is important to ensure there is a plan for an emergency. Decide how you will deal with the spare key. It should be readily available should the lock need to be removed in a hurry. Keep the spare key in a place that is far from kids or animals getting access to it. The Queen, of course, should have a key in her own possession at all times. Encourage good personal hygiene, and he must be allowed to remove the device to wash properly. The last thing you and he wants is an unwanted infection because of the device.

Set out a reasonable schedule that you both agree with. I always advise beginners to start with a few hours and build up from there. Perhaps the device can be put on for the night, then removed in the morning. Once you and your man are happy with the general performance and are comfortable in chastity, then your man can proceed to longer periods of wearing it.

Chastity and Infidelity

The chastity device is perfect for the few ways that infidelity can occur in a relationship—having affairs outside the relationship or constant daily masturbation. A man having sex with someone else without the Queen's permission or relieving himself alone at his computer, are both areas that are perfect to correct with male chastity. When a man's penis is locked, he is simply unable to do these things and his focus is solely on the Queen, where it needs to be. All of your man's energy should be used for serving you in your Female Led Relationship.

An effective way to evaluate your man's devotion to you is to assess his mannerisms and attitude prior to having sex. Then evaluate his attitude and behavior once again after you let him put his penis into your precious vagina and have an orgasm. You will often find that before you have sex with him, he is affectionate, loving, appears to be totally centered on your desires. After allowing him to have sex with you, he becomes removed, detached, and not concerned about your needs anymore.

He's ready to pick up the remote and watch the ball game or play video games on the computer, even if you would prefer that he cuddle with you for an hour after sex. Unacceptable. During male chastity, this may be a great time to use this practice to shape and change bad behaviors. Keep it light, but encourage him to satisfy your needs only when he is wearing his cage. When he has been released, give him the treat to have some freedom to do what he wants. Some Queens allow their men to remove the cage and enjoy having nights off where they can indulge in masturbation or go out with their friends without being constricted.

Female Led Relationship

Remember, your main purpose in locking him in a Male Chastity Cage is to train him that he exists for you to use him for all the pleasure that you desire, and he has no entitlement to any pleasure other than the pleasure of serving his goddess. Remember that Love & Obey Male Chastity and Orgasm Denial is designed to keep him constantly aroused and horny, so he will do whatever you want because he is always secretly hoping that you will allow him out to have intercourse with you and have an orgasm. When you keep him aroused and on the verge of thinking he's going to be allowed to have sex and get a sexual release, you will find that your man is willing to do whatever you want, not only sexually, but also any chores you want done around the house.

You must convince him until he truly believes that if he does what you command, then maybe you will allow him to have sex with you and have an orgasm. As always, your number one priority is always your pleasure and satisfaction at all times. You must not under any circumstances worry about giving a man sexual gratification unless he has given you all the pleasure and satisfaction that you desire. He should have truly pleased you with his behavior by doing everything you have asked him to do and fully servicing your sexual needs. In a true Female Led Relationship, the male's needs are always secondary to the needs and desires of the female.

Male Chastity and Daily Life

One of the easiest ways to get him accustomed to wearing the cage is to put it on while you are spending the day together to ensure there won't be any unforeseen problems that might arise from having him wear the device for longer than he's been previously used to. You can do it for an entire weekend and see how he copes with wearing it in daily life.

From there, it's a simple step to progressing to wearing it at work. Maybe it's an early morning ritual. As he goes about the day, he will be intimately reminded of you and your power over him, and it should make for some excitement throughout his day, causing him to be electrified when he returns home. Hopefully he can remain focused. The power of female led is introducing it as a regular part of life. Many men have admitted that although female led began in the bedroom, they welcomed FLR when it became a natural part of life. Male chastity is the same. The entire idea that your man is 100 percent devoted to you and is willing to show his devotion each and every day will be arousing to you both. But reinforcement, practice, leadership, and control will be necessary and you, the Queen, must take the reins and the responsibility of directing the process.

It is essential to set the rules in advance, preferably write them down, and stick to them at all times. This chastity contract will allow both parties to understand their roles and how far they can go. Both the keyholder and the caged partner must be comfortable with the contract, as well as the duties and responsibilities assigned to them. BDSM is all about submission and control, so the set of rules might even add an aura of seriousness to the game. The master-slave relationship will become official, and both sides can step into their roles with ease. Also, it's a good way to ensure that there will be no ad hoc changes and deviations that can ruin the pleasure. The rules can be as outrageous as you wish, but they have to be followed. Safety is crucial, and you don't want anyone to get hurt or be uncomfortable.

Playing Erotic Games

Now that he is used to chastity in daily life, it's time to explore some exciting ways to spice things up. Making long-term chastity can be exciting and rewarding for both of you. Male chastity should not change your sex life. Rather, it can be a great addition and should enhance it. Now, he just needs to focus on your pleasure first, then you can decide if he has an orgasm. One method that couples have chosen is for your man to tease, massage, perform oral sex, and only when you are fully satisfied should he be released from his cage. If he's been a "Bad Boy," then he may have to stay in his cage while all he does is pleasure you for the night. You can also add the use of your dildo while he gives you oral sex, since he won't be able to use his penis. The important part of all of this is that he must submit to your wishes.

Some games include:

Hide and Seek

This is one of the classics that never loses its allure. The idea is to hide the key and get the wearer to find it within a certain period of time. The search parameters can be anything from a single room to the entire house, although we would recommend a smaller area. If the quest is successful, your man can be free for a while and maybe get a juicier reward. If they don't find the object, they can get extra time on their lock period or simply wait for another opportunity to play. You can also play hide and seek and when you find your man, he gets to be locked up. This gives him extra motivation to hide well.

Teasing

The Key Holder teases her man by stimulating him in various ways. He is strictly forbidden from having an orgasm, regardless of how explicit the stimulation gets. You can do this while he is locked or before he is to be unlocked. An essential part of the game is that he must not ejaculate no matter how aroused he gets. It's a practice of self-control. If he manages to control himself, he can get a reward. Anything from the reduction of the lock period to a proper orgasm is good. Add some spanking or bondage to really spice things up.

Risk and Reward

In this game, you should give your man a list of tasks or challenges that they must complete to receive a reward. It can be anything from simple errands to more complicated missions. While it's nice to have him do the housework, you might consider assigning him sexual duties, such as oral pleasure or dildo penetration. It just adds some extra kink, and he can combine compliance with self-discipline.

Animal Kingdom

Your man needs to act out as different animals. The better his acting, the faster he is released from chastity. This is particularly funny if he has to act like a donkey by making hee haw sounds. Or mimic a pig or a gorilla. The idea is to be light and fun. The more we can laugh and keep sex light, the more interesting it becomes.

CHAPTER 13

Male Chastity in a Female Led World

S o why is male chastity so important to the female led world? In a Female Led Relationship, men become devoted, loving, obedient, and faithful as they dedicate servicing their loving female authority. He lives to serve his Queen, and he finds purpose in making her happy. What he gets in return is a strong alpha female who takes the lead and makes it her mission to do everything she can to be the Queen. It is a two-way street.

There are many levels to a Female Led Relationship:

1. The lowest level of an FLR has the woman with a limited amount of control and takes the lead on some decisions, but not all. Her dominance could also spill over into the bedroom, which can make for a more exciting sex life.

2. In the next level of a Female Led Relationship, the woman's role as the dominant partner begins to get a little more serious. She will start to call the shots on more areas of the relationship, and also dominate her man in the bedroom more. The man may take on more traditionally "female" roles in the relationship, such as taking care of the household.

3. At the third level of an FLR, the relationship will revolve around the woman's needs and desires. The man's actions will be centered around pleasing their woman. She can dictate most of what her man does and have the final say on most decisions.

4. The most extreme level of a Female Led Relationship sees the man act as a servant for their partner. The woman has complete control over her partner and the relationship will most likely have a dominatrix-submissive dynamic.

Chastity can occur at any level. At the first level of FLR, you, the Queen, may be just starting out and as such, she may request that her man simply do Chastity and some edging for one night. In higher levels of FLR the Queen can make male chastity a prolonged act or make it part of daily life and the female led contract. Many critics of FLR complain that the woman is going to take advantage of the man and this simply is not the case. Two people in a relationship only want the best and they both are willing to sacrifice for the sake of the relationship. The sacrifice that must be made by the woman is that she must, above all else, take the leadership role and guide the day to day. The sacrifice that men must make is they follow her lead and be as supportive as possible. When both people are involved 100 percent, the relationship thrives. Where they begin to unravel is when there is loss of interest, boredom, monotony, communication breakdown, and lack of sexual satisfaction.

Chastity is important because a man's body is no longer his own. In FLR, the man has become under the female's control, and it is the dominant female who must permit a man to join his body to his woman's or another body.

In female led life, your man has no right to demand or control sex. You control that privilege and male sexual gratification is given at your discretion. Disrespect the Queen, put her down or put her in a bad mood, then he is not likely to be rewarded. Some take it a step further to administer punishment. In a loving Female Led Relationship, it is the responsibility of the Queen to take note when the relationship is off course and to provide training and direction for the man, but it is the man's responsibility to follow her lead and that includes male chastity and orgasm control if that is what has been agreed on.

In other words, male chastity is a part of a Female Led Relationship. Love & Obey makes it clear that sex beyond the boundaries of the dominant female's established boundaries and sanctioned sex is simply off limits. To have sex outside those bounds is to commit an offense against your Loving Female Authority and requires strict discipline as found in my book *Spanking: The Erotic Guide to Relationship Discipline*. Obedience and Male Chastity within a Female Led Relationship, which men refrain from sex except with his dominant female's permission, is just one of those basic rules that keeps you inside the FLR community. Any other kind of sex is simply disobedience and must be punished.

A female led male in chastity must accept that his only purpose in life is to satisfy his woman in every way including sex and his only sexual satisfaction comes from giving his woman pleasure. Wearing a chastity device each and every day tells him that his devotion is for the Queen. Ladies, you want this kind of attention and focus on the relationship and on you from your man, which is why couples who follow a Female Led Relationship seem to have so much satisfaction that translates into everyday life.

Some people believe that all of this is just about how it improves the sex life, but female led and male chastity goes beyond just sex and what happens in the bedroom. While it is a powerful force for waking up sexual arousal and sex lives, the practical part of it relates to how you apply it to daily life. Make it a ritual. Set out a time to put on the cock cage at your command. Decide on the days you want him to wear it, maybe at work, or when going out. It is important to make chastity part of daily life. The more accustomed he gets to being reminded that his purpose is to demonstrate his devotion, the better he becomes. I have found that re-enforcement of a role that does not come naturally to a man is crucial to shaping his behavior and making him 100 percent obedient.

Men who practice chastity remain faithful to their women and honor them by giving their Queens ownership of their bodies and minds.

For most men, sex in a relationship quickly becomes the central focus of the relationship. It clouds their judgment and stops them from seeing the superiority of the female on many levels beyond sexual. Men must learn to gauge the relationship by how intense the emotions and feelings are of love, obedience, and service to the female. Sex produces intense feelings and is a woman's most powerful tool to make a man feel complete devotion to her.

Men are accustomed to taking charge and getting their own way, particularly in sex or if they get angry. It is during times of outburst or disobedience that the Queen's reinforcement of who is really in charge becomes crucial. It is also at times like these that you could implement some discipline. Maybe after his outburst he needs to wear his cage to calm him down, and he may need some spanking or more chores. The Female Led Relationship and my books *Love & Obey* and *Real Men Worship Women* provide lots of instruction on how to deal with situations like this. Now, Queens have an additional method in male chastity at their disposal to use as you see fit.

Women should take caution in the mindset that "friends with benefits" and "one-night stands" will lead to lasting female led connections—it won't. Where these hookups work for men, they will do nothing for a woman who wants to create a lasting relationship in which your man worships you. A man cannot worship a woman if he knows nothing about her, except having sex with her on a casual basis. Male chastity only works for couples in a committed long-term relationship. What a woman decides to do is her choice, but analyze your long-term goal.

Many women and men spend their 20s and 30s in shallow relationships, then all of a sudden, by mid to late 30s, a woman wants a relationship. The switch becomes almost impossible and many women and men find themselves alone. Relationships take work and creating the right Female Led Relationship takes seeking the right partner, being in a committed union, and practicing the principles daily. However, having experienced both sides, I choose relationships and create the right Female Led Relationship or marriage any day. It's more interesting, and relationships are about learning and evolving. Something I did not think that single life offered me.

Male chastity presents the perfect opportunity to take a Female Led Relationship to a whole new level. Maybe you have him at the point of doing more chores, serving you properly in bed, or treating you like a Queen. Now is the time for him to show his ultimate devotion and be in chastity at your command. Not only will it excite him that you are taking things even deeper, but it will give both of you a new purpose and goals for your relationship.

During male chastity, the female controls her male's sexual functions, specifically his orgasm release and semen ejaculation. Fortunately, many men are aroused when they feel weak for a woman, when they need her, and when they want to be controlled by her. Therefore, many men agree to be placed in chastity and have their orgasms controlled. It is great for women that many men want to be emotionally and sexually mesmerized by a woman. It is a secret desire for many men that makes Male Chastity so popular. Even the most alpha man is most comfortable being sub-male to the woman he loves—it is the classic Knight Queen psychology at work.

It may seem odd at first, but the fact is the subordination of the male to the female is based on the entire ritual of courting and marriage Whether this subordination is made explicit, like in a Female Led Relationship, or done covertly by shrewd women in male led relationships. It is up to the woman, as is virtually everything else that is handled, but today more women are empowered and opting for Female Led Relationships simply because women can set clear expectations and rules. Plus, and this is critical, women also set the sexual agenda after the first fevered weeks of courting and the "honeymoon phase."

For many women, controlling the sexual activity in a marriage is unconscious, but most women restrict their husband's sexual access from a very early stage in marriage. He may want sex three times a day, every day, but very few wives are willing to accommodate this sort of sexual gluttony. Especially because this type of man is still focused on his pleasure and that makes the sex become less pleasurable for the woman as time goes on. The great thing about a Female Led Relationship is that the focus shifts toward the woman.

Ironically, the woman may now want sex three times a day, every day, and the man has to keep up or be cuckolded.

Male Chastity can really set the rules quickly. Making sex "special" and not "every day" is a beginning. Using sex as a reward—the blow job for the completion of the honey-do list—and limiting penetration to a few times a month gradually transfers some sexual control to the wife. Every woman knows that a horny man is an attentive man. So male chastity is the "Holy Grail" of ways to keep a man horny and attentive. It is also a very good place to begin training a husband because, and here is a tiny secret, while men may think they want sex all the time, if they are allowed to have sex all the time, they quickly find out they aren't a stud.

In reality, it is the woman who can have sex many times a day, and even with many men without fatigue and ability to perform. So, usually from an early stage in any marriage, even a woman in a male led marriage who does not think of herself as a dominant wife will take charge in the bedroom. So why not be open about it and declare your female led lifestyle demands upfront? If he wants to have sex, he needs to agree to Love & Obey you.

The Female Led Relationship is instrumental in sorting out issues with power in relationships of which negative power dynamics can lead to the destruction of a marriage or relationship. There are two types of relationship dynamics that can result from negative power imbalances within the relationship: demand withdrawal and distance pursuer.

The demand-withdrawal dynamic occurs when one partner is the "demander" who seeks change, discussion, and is in constant search of a resolution to issues within the relationship—while the other partner is withdrawn, seeking to avoid the issues. According to a study conducted by Lauren Papp from the Department of Human Development and Family Studies, University of Wisconsin, and Chrystyna Kouros and E. Mark Cummings, both with the Department of Psychology at the University of Notre Dame, the demand/withdrawal dynamic has been linked with spousal depression and is a powerful predictor of dissatisfaction in the marriage and divorce.

Their findings also established a pattern of gender-bias within relationships that had the demand/withdrawal dynamic, with women predominantly being the "demanders" and men predominantly being "withdrawn." The fact that a Female Led Relationship requires the active participation of both people and establishes the Queen as the leader from the start, goes a long way to preventing this negative dynamic.

The distancer pursuer dynamic is explained as such: one person known as the pursuer tries to achieve and maintain a certain degree of intimacy with their partner, the distancer, who considers this affection to be "smothering."

In this unhealthy dynamic, the closer the pursuer wants to be, the more resistant, defiant, and withdrawn the distancer can be. This is considered to be very similar to the "demand/withdrawal" dynamic, however, with distance pursuer relationships, the struggle is over a deeper connection and less about who has more power. The distancer would imagine the issue in the relationship to be the "neediness" of their partner, and the pursuer would feel their partner has been cold and potentially even purposefully destructive by withholding affection.

Many women do experience this dynamic with men who tend to be much more submissive and needy. But a woman who enjoys taking the lead almost needs a man who tends to be the pursuer and, in this regard, it can be what keeps the relationship so strong. So, whereas in traditional patriarchal relationships this dynamic can present challenges, it works in a Female Led Relationship.

Two separate researchers of negative power imbalances in relationships, Dr. John Gottman and E. Mavis Hetherington, have both concluded that couples who are seemingly stuck in one of these negative power dynamics were at a very high risk for divorce. A Female Led Relationship offers a positive power struggle. According to psychiatrist Kurt Smith, a positive power struggle is one that ultimately results in the growth of the relationship. While the struggle is still a struggle, by the end of it, you will have reached an understanding of which lines can be crossed, which cannot, and how much each partner is able to compromise.

CHAPTER 14

How Chastity Keeps the Sexual Desire Alive

T he main reason we spend so much time focused on relationships and ways to improve them is because they have the power to affect our lives in such a dramatic way. In the Harvard study on successful aging, I was delighted to find that a good relationship was an extremely important factor found to affect aging. "The surprising finding is that our relationships and how happy we are in our relationships has a powerful influence on our health," said Robert Waldinger, director of the study, a psychiatrist at Massachusetts General Hospital, and a professor of psychiatry at Harvard Medical School. "Taking care of your body is important, but tending to your relationships is a form of self-care too. That, I think, is the revelation."

This demonstrates the effect of a great relationship on our health and lives. Part of a great relationship and marriage is great sex and sexual desire. So, I thought it important to analyze what affects sexual desire and helps to keep things exciting. In the *Journal of Sex Research*, published online in March 2018, Kristen Mark and Julie Lasslo present a systematic review of 64 studies on sexual desire in relationships spanning three decades.

The top five factors that either help or hinder our experience of sexual desire:

1. Expectations

Our interest in sex naturally ebbs and flows over the course of a long-term relationship. Researchers have reliably found that individuals who accept these fluctuations as normal and natural are more sexually satisfied. They are able to view the changes as understandable rather than problematic, which seems to help them weather the potential storm. In contrast, individuals who do not hold this perspective report greater worry and stress when they hit a sexual slump, consequently resulting in a negative impact on their sexual satisfaction. Chastity helps to manage those periods of flow because when the Queen is controlling her man's orgasm and he is in Chastity, the relationship is still sexually charged, though no actual sex may be happening. When he is finally allowed out of chastity, this is when things can heat up and having sex becomes exciting and adventurous.

Expectations about sexual desire were also found to extend into the research on desire discrepancies when one person has more sexual desire than their partner. That is, when couples acknowledge that it's normal even expected for individuals to want different frequencies of sexual activity and/or want sex at different times, they are more equipped to deal with it.

2. Autonomy

While feeling close and connected to a partner is crucial for relationship satisfaction, there is a downside to losing your independence. A number of studies have documented the importance of having some autonomy in our relationships in order to increase sexual desire and passion. It is important to take time to enjoy things that we like separately, and it gives us the breathing room to see our partner and appreciate them from a distance. Autonomy also gives us the space to experience our thoughts and feelings separately from our partner. This dynamic has been found to increase relationship satisfaction and, indirectly, sexual desire. When the Queen assumes the role as leader, she still has to manage the household, her careers and all other factors. The same is true for the man. Just because he is in hastity does not mean he cannot have his time in his man cave or with his friends. Couples always need some time alone without their partners.

3. Responsiveness to Partner

In relationships, we tend to be aware of our partner's needs and wants. The difference maker, according to research, is what we decide to *do* with that information. When we are particularly motivated to please a partner or make our partner happy, sexual satisfaction and sexual desire tends to follow. That includes being motivated to have sex when our partner wants it even if we're not so much in the mood, or trying something new that our partner is interested in because we know it would make them happy. The key is that our motivation is a relationship-enhancing one. Chastity presents a perfect way to always be attentive and responsive to each other. The Queen focuses her attention daily on her man, and she becomes the object of his desire. Responsiveness naturally increases in this type of relationship.

4. Self-Expansion

Self-expansion is the concept of embracing opportunities for growth. When it comes to sex, this can mean anything from trying new sexual positions, having sex in different locations or at various times of day, or wearing something a little out of the ordinary.

Across several studies, couples who report higher levels of sexual desire also report making the effort to try something new and different, no matter how small, to keep things interesting and fresh in the bedroom. The idea is to embrace your sexual interests and grow alongside your partner. This also helps avoid sexual monotony and routine. This is where Chastity helps to inject that sexual excitement and it's something new to explore, which can enhance the relationship or marriage.

5. Egalitarianism

Research has found that when couples experience higher egalitarianism, in that they contribute about equally to the relationship, sexual desire is also higher. In a Female Led Relationship and chastity, both people are contributing. When the Queen is focused on controlling her man, and he is focused on complete devotion, the sense of egalitarianism in the relationship is fulfilled.

It is believed by many that sexual desire plays an important role in romantic love, and that it may be an extremely important factor in strengthening the interpersonal dynamic of romantic relationships. Whereas women tend to consider love and emotional intimacy as high-ranking goals of sexual desire, men are more likely to consider sexual activity as the primary goal of sexual desire. Male chastity satisfies both because women are more likely to be sexually satisfied when they are pleasured more and men are happier when sexual activity increases.

In Sternberg's triangular theory of love, the three components of love are intimacy, passion, and decision commitment. All three are necessary for success in relationships and marriages. Sternberg says that intimacy refers to "feelings of closeness, connectedness, and bonding," passion refers to "the drives that lead to romance, physical attraction, sexual consummation, and related phenomena in loving relationships." And decision commitment means different things, "the decision that one loves another and one's commitment to maintain that love."

The two main types of love in relationships and marriage are passionate love and companionate. Passionate is a state of attraction and increased preoccupation with a specific person and may be described as obsessive love or infatuation. Passionate love is defined as a state of intense longing for union with another being in love. This intense feeling is characterized by the experience of great emotional highs and lows, and when it is reciprocated through union with the beloved, it can lead to feelings of euphoria, exhilaration, fulfillment, and ecstasy. Companionate love is a much less intense form of love, where desire for proximity and resistance to separation become less urgent. This form of love is influenced by feelings of attachment, commitment, and intimacy but is much less anxious than passionate love, and typically nurtures feelings of security, care, and comfort.

Romantic love strengthens the connection and bond we have with our partner. Studies with neuroimaging and romantic love have shown activation in regions of the brain, such as the amygdala, hippocampus, prefrontal cortex, hypothalamus, and ventral tegmental area (VTA). These structures are part of the reward circuitry that is linked to sex, food consumption, and drug use. Jacqueline Olds, a Harvard Medical School professor, says that when we are falling in love, chemicals associated with this circuit produce a variety of physical and emotional responses, such as racing hearts, sweaty palms, flushed cheeks, anxiety, and intense feelings of passion.

Being love-struck also releases high levels of dopamine, a chemical that gets the reward system going. It is widely known that the neuropeptide, oxytocin, is released during love and sex. The hormone has a role in pregnancy and nursing and is released during sex, making couples feel closer to one another. Regions that induce vasopressin are also activated during love and are often linked to behavior that produces long-term, monogamous relationships.

Dr. Helen Fisher of Rutgers University believes that oxytocin and vasopressin interfere with the dopamine and norepinephrine pathways, which might explain why passionate love fades as attachment grows. What is important is that in long-term relationships and marriages, there is an evolution of all of these types' phases but Female Led Relationships and adding new things, like male chastity and changing the dynamic in the relationship even after years of being together, can ignite more passion, excitement, or some romance that was lost.

CHAPTER **15**

The Spiritual Side of Male Chastity

Male Chastity represents an opportunity to explore the spiritual side of sex through Tantric Sex. Tantric is an ancient practice with Buddhist and Hindu origins. Tantra means "woven together." The idea is the metaphor of weaving man and woman together through the physical body. It also relates to the concept of weaving together the physical and the spiritual. Tantra uses the breath, as do other yogic practices, to engage mindfulness. It allows for a heightened awareness of both partners' emotional and spiritual states during the act of lovemaking.

Tantra also embodies the metaphor of weaving the human to the divine. The practice is meant to allow couples to become one with the god-state, the act of love likened to worshiping your lover as your temple. The act of tantric lovemaking inspires a sacred bond, by heightening intimacy to a divine level. Tantra also increases awareness of our own bodies, our own spiritual connection to sex. Through worship of the sacred bond of love, many tantric lovers experience extreme orgasms. These orgasms are powerful, and in some cases, can last for hours. This is generally the realm of experienced tantric couples, however, and it's important to remember that prolonged orgasm is not the point of the practice.

One popular tantric method is Karezza. Some prefer to take a toned down, spiritual, tantra-like approach to orgasm denial. Karezza involves prolonging or completely denying orgasms. It is a slow and sensual way of having sex that entirely removes climax from the sexual equation, leaving space for emotional connection and heightened affection. This is perfect for male chastity, which can involve orgasm control, orgasm denial, or semen retention. The karezza method has ancient spiritual roots but began to be widely established in the modern era with the publication of OB/GYN Alice Bunker Stockham's 1903 book *Karezza: The Ethics of Marriage.* Stockham coined the term karezza, which she took from the Italian word *carezza*, meaning "caress." The intent behind the karezza method is to deepen the sexual and emotional connection, according to certified clinical sexologist Randi Levison. The practice "teaches couples to focus on the entire being, not just a body part," she says. "It's all about relaxing and being in the present moment." The practice has also been known by the Latin name *coitus reservatus*, although this is slightly different from true Karezza because *coitus reservatus* only involves the penetrative partner withholding from orgasm while encouraging the receptive partner to still have them. This is in line with male chastity. You, the Queen, will have your orgasms while your man must withhold his.

Like tantric sex, and other more sensual sexual practices, the Karezza method has gained popularity over the years with couples who find that it brings true intimacy and connection back into their relationships. As part of male chastity, adding this spiritual component not only transforms your relationship, but it can also serve to be combined with other spiritual practices. One couple admitted that they added it to Lent. When they have to restrict foods that they eat as part of Christian living, they add orgasm control. Just this practice of self-control has allowed them to weave their sexual life into spiritual and religious.

Karezza started out as an extremely spiritual practice in which the centrality of sex to spirituality wasn't shied away from. In his book *The Karezza Method*, J. William Lloyd writes, "Sex is very close to soul. Whoso touches sex touches the secrets and centers of life. The voice of sex, in its power, is as the voice of God." Lloyd believed that Karezza requires preparatory mental exercise. It requires first the understanding and conviction that the spiritual, the caressive (the tender side of the relation), is much more important, much more productive of pleasure than the merely sexual, and that throughout the whole relation, the sexual is to be held subordinate to this love side as its tool, its agent, its feeder.

Sex is indeed required to furnish all it has to the feast, but strictly under the leadership of and to the glory of love. Both of you should think more about your love than your passion and translate your sex-passion as much as possible into heart-passion. Stockham says, "Karezza signifies to express affection in both words and action in a union that is the outcome of deepest human affection, love's through controlled sexual union. It's more than just self-control, but mutual control where the penetrative partner helps the receptive partner and vice versa." The technique prolongs sexual pleasure to the point of achieving mystical ecstasy. In this practice, orgasm is separated from ejaculation, making possible enjoyment of the pleasure of sexual intercourse without experiencing seminal ejaculation, while still experiencing orgasm. One purpose of Karezza is the maintenance, and indeed, intensification of desire and enjoyment of sexual pleasure within the context of relationships. Stockham believed that by eliminating the ejaculation and controlling it, the body gets a chance to recover and makes sexual sessions much more explosive.

Kalman Andras Oszlar writes, "Inasmuch as sexual togetherness is not limited into the physical world and does not mean quick wasting of sexual energies, by this we give free way to higher dimensions in the relationship." Affected by this, we may get into the state of flow, and in the course of this, the couple charges up with energy while with focused attention. The couple is submerging in that in which they are having pleasure. This state of mind connects with the achieved beneficial effects by tantric restraint and transformation. The flow experience is an entirely focused and motivationally intensified experience wherein the course of this, you and your man can entirely focus and properly command their feelings for the best performance or learning.

Tantric Sex

The three major keys to moving energy in tantra are breath, sound, and movement. Using these three keys, you can practice "running" your sexual energy throughout your body, whether you're engaged in sensual play or alone, and you can amp it up until it spills over into energetic orgasm. It can be such a profound and empowering aspect of connecting with your own innate sensuality. Steps to begin to get into the Tantric sex mood include getting prepared and creating the kind of space you'd like to be in to have any other kind of orgasm.

Foreplay can be anything you want it to be—oral, a massage, taking a shower together. But whatever you do, make sure you and your partner are fully present. Sit in front of your man. Look into each other's eyes. Start to move your bodies slightly as you breathe. After five minutes, start to touch each other sensually, taking turns massaging each other's arms, legs, neck, and other parts. After another five minutes, begin to kiss—and only kiss. Focus on every physical sensation you're feeling in the moment.

You both need to go within. Turn your attention inward, closing the eyes to signal to the mind that it's time to relax and let go. Open up the breath. Take some long, deep breaths to start, relaxing your entire body. Let the breath melt through any tension anywhere inside you. Then move into circular breathing, with no pause between the exhales or inhales. Connect to your sensuality. Focus your attention at the level of the genitals; connect to the quality of pleasure and eroticism within you. Fantasizing and caressing the whole body can help get you in the mood. Massage is vital to tantric sex, but not just any massage. Schedule a block of time and take the time to explore your man's body and vice versa.

The Yoni massage is a tantric massage technique designed to allow the Queen to relax and receive pleasure. *Yoni* is a Sanskrit word for the vagina, meaning "Sacred Space" and the vagina is viewed with the utmost love and respect. Yoni massage focuses on pleasure for the vagina while the Queen can focus on all the sensual pleasure. While your man is in chastity, he can focus on giving you a Yoni massage as an alternative to intercourse. Tantric sex is great for male chastity because it involves delayed or controlled orgasms but tantra involves much more than just orgasms. Holding off on orgasm relates to the concept of channeling sexual energy through the body, instead of releasing it through climax. Tantric couples often tout the benefits of retaining this energy as far as increased physical power and stamina—many will tell you that it feels incredible.

The goal of Tantra is to remain mindful of every sensation during the encounter, both in the context of giving and receiving. By staying mindful and basking in the experience itself, you build intense energy and affinity for your partner. This is where the intimacy is created and where the bonding takes place. Harnessing sexual energy is thought by many to be vital to our physical health. Sex can help regulate the stress response and increase serotonin levels. By giving and receiving during sex, you're not only giving your partner pleasure, you're giving the gift of health. Nothing could be deeper or more soothing than this level of caring.

Tantric Sex and Male Chastity

During the tantric experience, the acts of giving and receiving are considered sacred and each equally important as the other. Through the sacred act of giving, take your time and indulge your partner by giving pleasure. Connect with the spirit of selflessness and express your love for your man. In receiving, you give yourself the gift of pleasure and enable your man to connect with his own giving spirit. By allowing him to pleasure you, he has the opportunity to express all the love they have for us in their own way. By taking turns and being mindful of the sensations in each act, you are both able to connect with your own innate desire to please and be pleased. It is through these deep, mutual connections to the soul that intimacy is built. As the giver, encourage your man to take the time to explore your mouth while you focus on giving pleasure expressing your love. As the receiver, the Queen needs to allow her man to take his time kissing and exploring while you stay mindful of your physical sensations and give yourself wholeheartedly to both your partner and your role.

Tantric Sex and Orgasm Control

As we have seen previously, semen retention is part of male chastity and orgasm control. So, in tantric sex and male chastity, semen retention is a practice in which your man has an orgasm without ejaculating. Psalm Isadora, Tantric educator, said "By practicing semen retention, you can learn to move that sexual, orgasmic energy through your body so you feel the sensation of having an orgasm without actually ejaculating. This technique will help you transmute the urge to ejaculate into a rush of full-body orgasmic energy." To do it, Isadora said you must pull the energy from your genitals throughout the entire body using the "microcosmic orbit."

Here are the steps: As you're about to orgasm, inhale slowly. As you inhale, visualize pulling the orgasmic energy from your penis up the front of your body. You can also use a feather-light touch with your hands to help draw the energy upward. When the energy reaches the top of your head, exhale and send it back down. Let the pleasure wash over you.

She also talks about doing edging correctly. Edging is when you stop yourself from orgasming just before it happens, when you're right "on the edge" of coming. "We're not talking about trying to stop an orgasm when it starts. That's not safe," Isadora clarified. "We're talking about bringing yourself to the edge of an orgasm, pulling back, letting the orgasmic feelings move through your body, and then repeating the cycle over and over."

Here are the steps: When he is right on the metaphorical edge of hitting your climax, stop or slow the sexual activity, but stay aroused. Wait about 30 seconds, during which he might continue giving you another gentler form of stimulation, like soft touches along the thighs. Begin the more intensely stimulating sexual activity again. Repeat from step one until he is ready to climax. You can also use the microcosmic orbit technique described above to move the sexual energy upward. Every time you restart the sexual activity, you're getting a new powerful pulse of energy to move upward, such that it begins to feel like waves and waves of pleasure rippling up your body. When you finally release, the orgasm should feel like a stronger, fuller-bodied experience.

Cervical orgasm is one type of orgasm your man can help you with while he is in chastity. Cervical orgasms are achieved by stimulating the cervix. Some people describe these orgasms as feeling more fuller-bodied. It's possible that because the cervix is located at the very back of the vaginal canal, reaching it often involves deep penetration that totally fills up the vagina and even presses up further into the body internally. This "full" feeling might explain why cervical orgasms can feel so good. You can also use a sex toy to reach the cervix and stimulate it, usually through a thrusting motion. Importantly though, the cervix can be very sensitive and may even hurt when it's hit initially, so it's important to work up to cervical stimulation. Starting out with stimulating the clitoris and getting the vagina aroused and opened up is important, and it might help to have a regular clitoral orgasm first before trying for the cervical orgasm through penetration.

Leslie Grace, RN and sex educator, suggests that an energy orgasm can be really great for tantric experience. It involves separating the experience of an orgasm from the physical stimulation. The basic idea behind the energy orgasm is that we all have this potent stream of Eros within us—this sexual, creative, life force energy flowing and animating our being at all times. This flow is literally available to us continuously, but unfortunately, it's currently not socially acceptable to fall into an orgasmic swoon in public at any time of the day or night, so we generally hold our energy systems kind of tightly and keep our minds firmly in control of the situation.

Here are the steps: Lie back comfortably with your knees bent and feet on the bed or floor. Take long, deep breaths to relax the entire body. Focus on your genitals, visualizing yourself stimulating yourself slowly and sensually without actually doing it. Your man can hold one hand over your genitals and create a motion of moving the sexual energy from your genital area upward, starting with small strokes and then building up to longer ones, reaching all the way up your body. In rhythm with your breathing and with his hand and energy movements, start to undulate and create a wavelike motion with your body. Make noise. Start out with soft moans and really start to let loose and get loud as the sexual energy begins to build. Increase the speed of your motions and sounds of your moans. You'll start to feel the pressure building. Keep going until you finally reach that orgasmic peak. The idea behind the energy orgasm is to let your mind go to allow the power of this orgasmic flow to come through.

To increase the tantric experience during your regular sex sessions, below are some tips for you and your man to implement during your regular sex sessions.

Start by bringing attention to the upper body. For the Queen with vulvas, nipple stimulation triggers the same pleasure network in the brain as clitoral stimulation. Having both happening at the same time can feel like a unifying, full-bodied experience. Dig your fingers into each other's back or scalps during penetration—anything to draw the attention upward and connect the arousal from the bottom to the top of the body. Move the body. Rock the body and create wavelike motions with your hips, back, shoulders, and head. Keep your whole body engaged in the experience of pleasure.

Barbara Carrellas, Tantric Educator, says, "Most people tend to hold their breath or breathe in a quick, shallow, panting sort of way during sex. But that type of breathing is limiting. The more you breathe, the more you feel, and the more sexual energy you raise. Think of your body as a 30-

gallon container. If you breathe very little during partner sex or masturbation, you raise very little energy—perhaps the amount that might fill a coffee cup. If you breathe more fully and deeply than you usually do from the beginning of a sexual experience all the way through to orgasm, you fill up your entire container. With all that energy, you are much more likely to experience a longer, deeper, expanded, extended orgasm."

Lastly, make lots of noise. We know that sounds can stimulate different parts of the body. But in tantric sex practices, using your voice is thought to be another way to move your energy. Using a lower-pitched voice moves energy down your body toward your genitals, and using higher pitches moves energy upward. Try using your sexual noises as part of how you're drawing sexual energy upward in your body to get that full-body feeling. Tantric sex requires you both to connect to non-physical sensations. The orgasm is not just a physical experience. It also involves a release of tension and expansion of energy flowing through the body and mind, and connecting you to spirit, your full-body orgasm experience might include a physical tingling accompanied by a huge emotional release and a feeling of oneness with nature. Barbara Carrellas says, "Tingling, vibrating, expansive sensations in nongenital body parts, gigglegasms, crygasms, blissgasms, and feelings of expansiveness, peak experience, peace, and connection are all common."

Benefits of Tantra

Here are all the benefits of Tantra that you and your man can experience:

- Awakening your sexual energy to flow freely within your body.

- Accessing your fullest pleasure and desire.

- Tuning into subtle energy.

- Discovering full-body and/or multiple orgasms.

- Experiencing a new level of heart connection with your partner's profound sense of intimacy and loving presence.

- Longer lovemaking sessions, relaxation, and a quality of spaciousness.

- Enhanced communication and communion.

Holistic mind-body-spirit connection with yourself and with your partner.

CHAPTER 16

Best Positions Male Chastity

There are many positions you can experiment with when you are exploring tantric sex and male chastity. But we will introduce some of the more popular ones. The idea behind the classic tantric sex position represents the union of Shiva and Shakti, the two divine energies of masculine and feminine. The base partner representing Shiva, who is energetically or physically penetrative, your man sits cross-legged on a pillow in the "holding" position while the other partner, the Queen, representing Shakti who is energetically or physically receptive, can either drape her legs over her partner's legs with her butt on the bed or a pillow or can fully sit in her partner's lap. Your man's arms should go around the Queen's waist and her arms on the shoulders. Your heads can be cheek to cheek, or you can touch forehead to forehead. This position aligns the chakras of the partners and allows for sexual energy to move upward along the spine. Sitting while facing each other, or having your man on his knees pleasuring you while you lay back, can be great for this type of energy exchange. You want to be able to gaze into each other's eyes as you savor all of the sensations. Facing each other involves the man sitting on the floor with legs out in front of him, leaning back on his hands while the woman sits on his lap facing him with her legs extended in front of her and leaning back on her hands. What's great about this position is if your man is wearing his cock cage, it's a comfortable position to tease and experience the sensations of tantra.

You can also remove his cage and request that he remain in chastity without it. Once you come into alignment, start by taking a few deep, slow breaths together, synchronizing your breathing. Then begin to move together in slow undulations, arching, swirling in circles, finding a flow and a rhythm that feels delicious, activating your sexual energy together. The base partner, your man "gives" to you, the Queen, on top who is "receiving" that energy up into their body. Connect with your breath to expand the pleasure and sexual energy throughout the entire body, lighting up every cell with that life force. You can try staying with smaller, subtle movements or get as vigorous as you like, but either way, use your breath to draw orgasmic energy from your pelvis up the spine and up to your third eye—the spot between your eyebrows—or crown the top of the head and beyond.

Another position is the man kneels by the side of a bed or chair and the Queen, sitting on the bed or chair, wraps her legs around his waist so that he can serve you orally or eventually penetrate you. This position allows for lots of mindful touching and caressing while giving your man control over both penetration and movement.

Here are some tips for both you and your man to heighten the experience:

- Smile, especially when making eye contact.

- Make skin-to-skin contact.

- Give approval with smiles or compliments.

- Look into your partner's eyes for a few moments.

- Listen to your partner intently.

- Synchronize your breathing with your partner's.

- Kiss your partner with your lips and tongue.

- Cradle or gently rock your partner's head or torso.

- Hold or spoon your partner in stillness for at least half an hour.

- Make wordless sounds of contentment or pleasure in front of your partner.

- Stroke your partner with the intent to comfort them.

- Massage your partner, especially on the feet, shoulders, or head.

- Hug your partner with the intent to comfort them, lie with one ear over your partner's heart to hear their heartbeat.

Suck or touch your partner's nipples and breasts and place your hand gently over your partner's genitals with the intention to comfort them.

CHAPTER **17**

Male Chastity and BDSM

B DSM means Bondage, Discipline, Dominance, Submission, Sadism, and Masochism. BDSM includes an extremely wide range of activities, from light paddle spanking and dominant submissive role-playing to bondage parties and pain play. Male chastity comes out of BDSM with the master slave dynamic. Many couples add other aspects of BDSM like spanking, bondage, and blindfolding with male chastity. Maybe while he is in chastity, the Queen can administer a light fun spanking, or tie him up or blindfold him while you tease him. Tease and denial are great to add.

Male chastity involves a man voluntarily surrendering authority over the most intimate part of his body, placing it entirely at the whim of his keyholder until she sees fit to release him again. Doing so is an act of submission on his part, acknowledging her to be the dominant party in their relationship, but it is far from being the only way in which he can submit to her will. Donning a pair of handcuffs or allowing himself to be tied up will render him similarly powerless, making more traditional bondage a popular accompaniment to chastity. The same psychological factors are at play—by ceding control of his body and its movements, he is no longer responsible for anything that might happen to him, allowing him to relax safe in the knowledge that, however harshly his mistress may treat him, there is absolutely nothing he can do about it.

You can introduce a little light bondage to your chastity play with anything that can tie his hands behind his back—a discarded stocking is perfectly sufficient, although a pair of handcuffs is better from both a practical and psychological point of view. For maximum effect, have him bound before you, remove his chastity device, and keep him that way until his cock is safely under lock and key again, emphasizing that one way or another he remains at your mercy.

Fantasy and role-playing are one of the most common forms of kinky sex and involves creating imagined scenarios, acting out fantasies, and wearing costumes. Fetishes. One out of four men and women are interested in fetish play, defined as treating a nonsexual object or body part sexually. Common fetishes include the feet and shoes, leather, or rubber. Male chastity can be added to many of these fetishes. Maybe he's into feet fetish. While your man is in chastity, he can spend some time worshipping your feet. Maybe you both can engage in role-playing and costumes. Have some fun teasing him in a sexy nurse costume or sexy superhero.

Voyeurism or exhibitionism. Watching someone undress or watching a couple have sex without their knowledge are common voyeur fantasies, while having sex in a public place is one form of exhibitionism and 35 percent of adults surveyed were interested in voyeurism. Male chastity can work with voyeurism. The Queen can place her man in chastity and have him watch her do a striptease. Or maybe your man becomes the stripper while the Queen takes a break.

Contrary to popular belief, the man who is submissive is never truly out of control.

Many people assume that a dominant, in this case, the Queen makes demands and orders at all times. Yes, this may happen once the relationship has been established and there is understanding within the dynamic. But there is a large element of trust that needs to be built within a relationship with a power dynamic. Even when forced to do something, it should be on the man's own free will. There should always be an out, exit, or safe words available. BDSM is all about placing your trust in another person. Your man decides to take on the role of surrendering control to you, the Queen who said, in a healthy BDSM relationship, Subs will ultimately decide when to start and stop. Carefully selected mechanisms, like safe words, provide him with control and agency. You need to implement this safety during male chastity, and communication is the key to keeping everything running smoothly. The last thing you want is for your man to resent you for forcing him to do something he's not into. So, consent from both of you is crucial.

Chastity fits into BDSM with erotic sexual denial. Erotic sexual denial is sometimes used by a dominant, the Queen, to increase their control over a submissive. Because the submissive is kept in a state of sexual need and vulnerability, they are more likely to take a compliant stance with the dominant; failure to comply can result in additional teasing or an extended period of denial, among other punishments, like time-out, spanking, and bondage. Some Queens will have their man assume the man-table position or attend to more chores than usual.

Orgasm denial practices can allow the dominant, the Queen to exercise control over many aspects of her man's life. As such, they are often though not always practiced as an extension or enhancement of a broader BDSM relationship, or as a means of establishing one. They can allow the dominant Queen to experience enjoyable and sometimes intensely craved feelings of sexual control and erotic power, and the submissive can enjoy intense feelings of sexual objectification and submission to the dominant. Orgasm denial can also be used to increase a submissive's tolerance for physical stimulation, as training in holding back the orgasm, or to allow the submissive to orgasm on command as a way to maintain a heightened state of sexual arousal in the submissive, or as a means of erotic humiliation desired by either the submissive or the dominant. Erotic humiliation can also help enforce the dominant's position in the relationship. Orgasm denial is often accompanied by other forms of erotic humiliation such as forcing the submissive to do chores, cross-dress, or consume bodily fluids. These can be used as punishments, as conditions for release, or simply at the discretion of the dominant.

Conclusion

Male chastity is growing and becoming more popular. The Female Led Relationship is only made stronger with the addition of male chastity as it is the ultimate sign of respect, love, and devotion. Male chastity serves to empower women and place them in the power position, which opens up the opportunity for real growth and evolution in the relationship. Male chastity simply deepens the emotional connection. Male chastity has been reported to transform relationships. Whether it is done with or without a device, it proves to be a powerful addition to a relationship or marriage.

The Queen assumes the position Key Holder, which makes her really feel more empowered as the "Guardian of the Penis." The man is the submissive, and through his willingness to be in chastity, he shows his ultimate devotion to service to his Queen. In a Female Led Relationship, the Queen is the ultimate leader and her man serves her as the supportive gentleman. Philosophers like Hegel show that the man's service is just as important to the relationship as the Queen's leadership, and in some cases even more important. The Queen can only be her best with the support of her man.

Male chastity has the ability to help to change some very destructive behavior like over-masturbation, infidelity, and patriarchal sex. It helps to regulate the sex and keep the focus on the Queen. Chastity requires the full consent of both the Queen and her man and should never be used as a manipulation tool or a vicious ply to severely punish the man. Men have actually been overwhelmingly obsessed with male chastity and many are eager to try it. Before beginning, it is important to set the ground rules and discuss it openly before proceeding.

Some couples may choose to add sex toys and other forms of BDSM, like spanking and bondage, which only serves to increase the excitement and adventure. Above all, the Queen and her man must show respect to each other while engaging in chastity, and it should only become part of a healthy committed relationship. Have fun with it, and use it as part of a strong Female Led Relationship. For more tips and guidance to create a successful female led life, get my other books in the *Love & Obey* series.